HORSE AND BUGGY DAYS ON HATCHET CREEK

MITCHELL B. GARRETT

HORSE AND BUGGY DAYS

ON HATCHET CREEK

UNIVERSITY OF ALABAMA PRESS

Second Printing, 1964

COPYRIGHT 1957 BY UNIVERSITY OF ALABAMA PRESS
DRAWER 2877, UNIVERSITY, ALABAMA
LIBRARY OF CONGRESS CATALOG CARD NUMBER 57-7179

CONTENTS

FOREWORD

I have had playmates, I have had companions,
In my days of childhood, in my youthful school days;
All, all are gone the old familiar faces.

CHARLES LAMB

IN THE SUMMER of 1949 my brother Warner and I paid a
day's visit to the rural community in which we were born
and raised, and which we had quitted more than half a century earlier. As we rolled along in our old Mercury sedan
over the roads, some of which in recent years have been
made passable for automobiles with high slung chassis, we
talked of familiar faces and of the radical changes " 'twixt
now and then."

Gone were the open forests of long leaf pines, whose
bare trunks once rose like slender columns to their tufted
tops in the sky. On the right hand and on the left, covering
the hills and abandoned plowlands, were dense groves of old-
field pines, good for nothing but paper pulp and possibly an
inferior grade of lumber. Overhanging the roads in the
swamps and lowlands was a tangled growth of juvenile oaks,
pines, hickories, blackgums, sweetgums, sourwoods, dogwoods,
huckleberry bushes, and sundry other vegetation, shutting out
the view and smothering the traveler. Where we expected to
find a familiar farmhouse, we sometimes found, instead,

a cultivated field or a patch of ground covered with rubble and brambles. Even when we did come upon a farmhouse that we were looking for, it was not as we remembered it, being surprisingly small, or disguised by painted weather-boards and a shiny metal roof, or rendered desolate and forlorn by the disappearance of the grove of stately oaks that once gave beauty, dignity, and shade to the surrounding area.

The few people whom we encountered along the way were friendly enough and easy to talk to; they responded to our inquiries with courtesy; but they were singularly un-interested in what the country looked like sixty years earlier. To them, two old men, riding backwards, as it were, with their faces turned toward the past, were of little importance: treat them kindly and let them pass on seemed to be the common sentiment.

As we were passing the old Goza place, Warner pointed to a house on the opposite side of the road, a house that I did not remember existed, and remarked: "Our old schoolmate, Isaac Chandler, lives there." So we sought Isaac out and the three of us had a long talk.

"Mitch, do you remember," Ike asked, "when you, my brother Tom and I trotted all the way one morning, three miles and a half, from our house to school?"

Yes, I remembered. I had gone home with the Chandler boys from school to spend the night with them. The next morning, bubbling over with youthful energy and excite-ment, we started back to school at a trot. Ike, being younger and smaller than Tom and I, fell far behind in the race; but we trotted on and left him wailing in anger and frustration. What nincompoops and heartless brutes small boys can sometimes be.

For an hour or more Warner and I swapped reminiscences with Ike and talked of this and that. Then we resumed our journey, smiling with pleasure at the follies and escapades of our joyful school days.

But when we reached the site of our school, we found only desolation. The schoolhouse was gone, even to the stones of its foundation. Gone, too, was the Primitive Baptist Church that once stood not fifty yards apart from it. Obliterated also was the well-beaten path to the spring that once bubbled up beneath an overhanging rock. The spring was silted up and transformed into a bog.

With a sense of melancholy akin to pain, I trudged from the site of the church up the gently sloping hillside, over rough footing, through prickly underbrush and saw-briers, to the graveyard where a score or more of good Primitive Baptists were laid to rest. After a diligent search among bushes and briers, I found the grave of my grandfather, which I easily identified by reason of the rough stone covering which my father, with loving hands and filial piety, built over it in the days of my youth.

Warner and I ate our picnic lunch at the site of the old mill. As we munched our sandwiches, our memories were full of the hours we once spent fishing and swimming in the old mill-pond and in the bowl-like pool just below the dam, often in hilarious companionship with other boys of the community. It was glorious fun to peel off our clothing and, naked as frogs, to dive from the springboard into the murky water of the pond and race upstream with all our flippers flapping.

But the old mill was there only in our memories. Years ago — nobody in the community seemed to remember when — one of those spring freshets for which Hatchet Creek was notorious lifted the barn-like structure off its foundations, crushed it like an eggshell and swept the debris onward toward the Coosa river. The old wooden dam may have survived the millhouse for a few years; but, left to decay, it could not long withstand the impact of the spring freshets. In its hunched-up back appeared a yawning and ever widening chasm, through which the impounded water escaped. Above the broken dam, in the deep silt on the banks of the narrow stream that was once the wide mill-pond, a lush growth of willows and other trees marked the return of the forest. Undernourished blackberry briers covered the space where farmers once hitched their sleepy mules and parked their light wagons while they waited for their turns of corn to be ground into meal.

"Let's go fishing," I suggested.

We scrambled down over the rough debris to the level of the pool below the dam. We adjusted our homemade tackle and baited our hooks with fishworms which we had brought along in a discarded tin can. For reasons best known to themselves the spot-tails and sun-perch, which were supposed to make the pool their special habitat, refused to take our bait; but, though we caught nothing, the hour spent was not without its compensations. How familiar was the odor of the mud, the decaying vegetable matter, and the warm creek water. In shaded nooks and eddies, mellow-bugs in large clusters floated on the surface of the water and broke into a frenzied dance when disturbed, just as they used to do. Gnat-catching insects which we boys used to call snake-doctors, probably distant cousins of the dragon-fly, flitted about and, lighting on overhanging twigs, hoisted their black wings like tiny sails. Occasionally a small water snake, hiding beneath the submerged rock, poked its head to the surface for a breath of fresh air. Down the creek a kingfisher announced his presence by his rattling cry.

It was all familiar and conducive to nostalgia.

As I sat musing on a broken sill of the old milldam, my senses assailed by the smells, sights, and sounds of the days of my childhood, the idea of writing a book some day, describing our way of life in the Hatchet Creek community sixty years ago, began to take shape in my mind.

It was a way of life well worth looking back on — no housing shortage, no fuel shortage, no atom bombs, no haunting fear of a third World War. Why not escape from the discomforts and worries of the present to the peace and simplicity of the past?

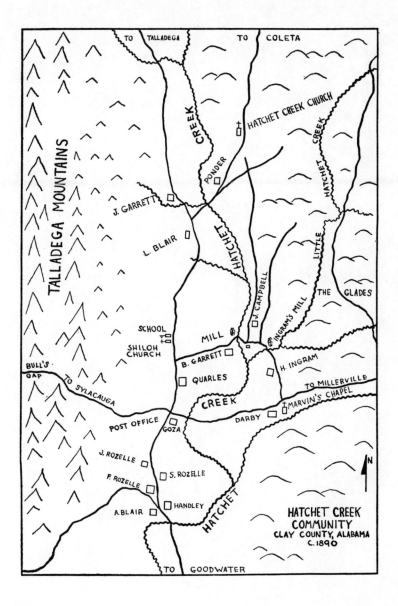

TO TALLADEGA

TO COLETA

TALLADEGA MOUNTAINS

CREEK

HATCHET CREEK CHURCH

PONDER

HATCHET

LITTLE HATCHET CREEK

J. GARRETT

L. BLAIR

J. CAMPBELL

INGRAM'S MILL

THE GLADES

SCHOOL

MILL

SHILOH CHURCH

B. GARRETT

QUARLES

H. INGRAM

BULL'S GAP

TO SYLACAUGA

CREEK

TO MILLERVILLE

MARVIN'S CHAPEL

POST OFFICE

DARBY

GOZA

J. ROZELLE

S. ROZELLE

N

F. ROZELLE

A. BLAIR

HANDLEY

HATCHET

HATCHET CREEK COMMUNITY
CLAY COUNTY, ALABAMA
C. 1890

TO GOODWATER

AN OVERALL VIEW

 IN MY YOUTH the Hatchet Creek community was, roughly speaking, six miles long and three miles wide. On the west was a range of mountains covered with long leaf pines, which moaned ominously when a storm was brewing. A north-south road, called, for want of a better name, the Goodwater-Talladega road, traversed the community parallel to the mountain range. Along the road passed the mail rider back and forth every day of the week except Sunday, serving the rural postoffices between Goodwater and Coleta, a distance of about fifteen miles. On the east were rolling hills skirted with farms and covered with long leaf pines. From its source far to the north Hatchet Creek, fed by numerous tributaries, meandered through the valley and disappeared in the south.

The mountain range and its foothills, being unfit for agriculture, remained public domain, the property of the Federal Government. But adjacent farmers did not hesitate to exploit this vast common at pleasure, using it as a free range for their domestic animals and divesting it of some of its finest trees for building purposes. Along the crest of the range ran the boundary line between Clay and Talladega counties. At Bull's Gap, about a third of the way up from the southern extremity of the community, a wagon road, steep and winding, crossed the mountain. There was a tradition that Old Hickory led his army through this pass in pursuit of the Creek Indians, whom he came up with and defeated at the Battle of the Horseshoe over on the Tallapoosa River.

The main axis of the community was the Goodwater-Talladega road. If you started at the southern extremity of the community and moved northward along the road, you would pass the homes of perhaps two-thirds of the population of Hatchet Creek.

On the left, at the far side of an oak grove, was the residence of Asa Blair. The main part of the house was constructed of logs — two large, box-like rooms separated by a hallway. At each end of the structure was a rock chimney with an enormous fireplace capable of accommodating logs six feet long. Appended to the main structure, and bearing the marks of a later date, were a porch and a small bedroom across the front, and a combination kitchen-dining room and a bedroom across the back, made of sawed materials. Covering all was a roof of hand-made boards rived with a froe. There were several log houses similar to this in the community, the main parts of which dated from frontier days.

Asa Blair had a kindly face, an impressive black beard, and a deep voice of a peculiar resonance. Dust-covered in his attic was a heavy sabre, the blade curving backward, which he wore with distinction as a cavalryman in the Civil

War. His farm of some two hundred acres contained rich bottom land for the production of corn, rolling hillsides for cotton, and extensive woodlands. For years he was justice of the peace and, as such, he could be seen on occasion carrying a small satchel, or grip, containing official papers, swung over his shoulder by a long leather strap. Because of his judicial office his neighbors frequently called him "Square." For years also he was clerk of the Primitive Baptist Church, and accepted without question the doctrine of election and predestination and the final perseverance of the saints.

The Lord blessed Asa Blair with bountiful harvests and prolific flocks and herds, and his good wife Phronie presented him with seven stalwart sons and one daughter.

On the right hand side of the road, directly facing the Blair residence, and also shaded by a grove of fine oaks, was the home of John Handley, a late comer to the community. His house was of modern construction, being made entirely of sawed materials. Mr. and Mrs. Handley were blessed with five lovely daughters and three sons. Whether predestined from the foundation of the world I can not say, but two of the Blair boys married two of the Handley girls.

A little farther along the road were the residences of the three Rozelle brothers, Frank, Sam, and John. Frank did a little farming, but his main business was store-keeping. In the grove of small trees between his residence and the road stood his store with its high, square façade. Whether he ever took an inventory of his stock is doubtful, but over the years a surprising variety of articles accumulated on his shelves, running the gamut from coffin tacks to chamber mugs.

Frank was a friendly man who knew all the children in the community by their first names and would not grumble when called upon to rise from his easy chair by the door and sell a penny's worth of candy. By family tradition he was a Methodist, but he could often be seen worshipping at the Primitive Baptist Church on the fourth Sunday of the month. He was a faithful Democrat; during Cleveland's second administration he kept the Hatchet Creek postoffice.

About Sam Rozelle there was nothing particularly distinctive, except that he had an alert countenance and a loud voice. He seemed to assume that the person to whom he was speaking was partially deaf.

In contrast to Frank and Sam, John, the oldest of the Rozelle brothers, was something of a "character." He was enthusiastic and loud-spoken, and his thoughts seemed to leap about like grasshoppers. He frequently left sentences half finished, puffed, gasped, raised his voice, took a new reef in his sail, and steered the conversation in a different direction. But despite his nervous temperament he was a substantial citizen, highly respected for his many fine qualities. He was a successful farmer; he owned and operated a steam-driven gin; and for several years he kept a pedigreed jackass for breeding mules.

The farms of the Rozelle brothers extended along the road for nearly a mile. In popular parlance this stretch of the road was called Rawsel Town, a corruption of the name Rozelle which was not greatly appreciated by its bearers.

The road now passed through a scope of woodlands and came out at the Goza place.

Tull Goza, a few years before I was born, served Clay county as tax collector, having been elected to that office by the voters of the Democratic party; but around 1888 he drifted away from his ancient moorings and became affiliated with what was soon to be called the Populist party. This shift of party affiliation cost him the good will of many of his neighbors, who looked upon Populism as something malodorous.

In personal appearance and temperament, Mr. Goza, as I remember him, was not unlike (whiskers and all) George Bernard Shaw — with ample apologies to that distinguished Irishman. At some time in his early life the wrist of his left arm was broken and never properly reset — perhaps a casualty of the Civil War. As a result of this misfortune, his left hand crooked inward at the wrist and remained fixed at almost a right angle to his forearm. Thus maimed he could not do much farming; but intermittently he kept a store and, during Cleveland's first administration and Harrison's, his wife was able to supplement the family income by keeping the Hatchet Creek postoffice. Mrs. Goza was a faithful member of the Primitive Baptist Church. Mr. Goza usually accompanied her when she attended divine worship, but one could easily detect from his listening attitude that he had little religious fervor. Perhaps his soul was vexed at the possibility that God had elected and predestined the Bourbon Democrats to be the dominant political party in the South.

The Quarles place came next on the road, the house standing at the far side of an oak grove.

John D. Quarles was originally a planter in Russell county. About a decade after the close of the Civil War he and his wife, with their seven sons and two daughters, trekked to the Hatchet Creek community, where an eighth son was soon born to them.

The Quarles house was a frame building which showed signs of having been rapidly put together for practical purposes. The main structure consisted of two square rooms at each end and a hallway in the middle, covered with a pyramidal roof. Two chimneys with double fireplaces furnished heat for the four rooms. There was a porch in front and another at the back. The combination kitchen-dining room was a separate building several steps in the rear of the "big house." At a convenient distance were the cribs and stables.

Mr. Quarles lost his wife in 1883 and followed her to the grave in 1888. One of his sons was already operating the farm and he continued to do so. As farm laborers he preferred Negroes, and always had two or three Negro families in his service. There was no "nigger quarter" on the farm, but a large bell bracketed at the top of a tall post signalized the periods of rest and labor. Negroes and mules were the distinctive characteristics of the Quarles farm.

The Quarleses were all highly respected citizens — moral, religious, and honest. They voted the Democratic ticket, joined the Missionary Baptist Church, and co-operated in all community activities. But their speech was somewhat distinctive: it closely resembled Negro dialect. Such words as corn and Negroes they pronounced "cawn" and "niggas," and when called on to speak their name they invariably said

"Quawls." The community accepted this pronunciation as the right one and never knew that there was any other.

About half a mile beyond the Quarles place, on the left hand side of the road, stood the Primitive Baptist Church, which bore the Biblical name Shiloh. The building stood on government land and was partially surrounded by a grove of blackjack, pine, and hickory. Here religious services were held on the fourth Saturday and Sunday of each month. A rough wagon road led to the top of a nearby hill where good Primitive Baptists, who had fought the good fight and finished the course, were laid to rest, to await the Resurrection Morn. Two flat rocks picked up on the mountainside, a small one at the foot and a larger one at the head, marked each grave.

Only a few steps from the church building stood an old dilapidated log schoolhouse, with a large rock chimney and fireplace at one end. About 1888 or 1889 this relic of frontier days was replaced by a more commodious frame structure in the form of a T, which was heated by a fireplace and a stove. To this school came the children of the whole community, from the south, east, and north. They all walked to school in the morning, some of them as far as three miles or more, and back again in the late afternoon, carrying their lunch pails.

For a mile north of the schoolhouse the road crept over low lying hills. Here the soil was reddish gray and subject to erosion. In consequence the farmers living along this stretch were not notably fat and prosperous. Then came the gradual descent into the bottomlands of Hatchet Creek and the Leroy Blair place.

Leroy Blair was a late comer to the community, having bought his farm in 1889 from Dr. Prickett, an indifferent farmer and country doctor, who had caught the western fever and wanted to migrate to Arkansas. With the coming of the Blairs — father, mother, seven sons, and one daughter — the old place began to take on a new look. The log house was doubled in length and size by the addition of a frame structure; cribs, stables, and fences were repaired or replaced; and fresh clearings were made in the fertile bottomlands. All this expenditure of labor necessitated log-rollings in the spring and house-raisings at various times of the year, when neighbors were invited to lend a hand, and were given enormous and appetizing meals for their pains.

With the assistance of his seven stalwart sons, Leroy Blair raised great crops of corn which he fed to mules, cows, and pigs, or sold to neighbors in the community. He was a stanch Democrat, a faithful member of the Primitive Baptist Church, and a good citizen.

Beyond the Leroy Blair place the road forked. The left hand prong was the continuation of the Goodwater-Talladega road. Still running roughly parallel to the mountain range, it crossed the John Garrett farm and continued on into Horn's Valley, another rural community. The right hand prong, which was the mail route now, crossed Hatchet Creek on a bridge and continued in a northeasterly direction to Coleta and beyond. On this prong, not far from the bridge, was the residence of William Ponder.

William Ponder, a widower and the father of a healthy son, married one of my father's sisters, Aunt Nettie, who at the time of the nuptials had attained the ripe age of sixteen. The Ponder house was a small frame structure on the top of a hill, from which point of vantage one could catch a sweeping view of the mountain range on the west. The water supply came from a well equipped with curb, windlass, and shelter at the foot of a hill. Uncle Bill, as I remember him, was a thin, elderly man, who sat on his tiny front porch in nice weather, with his hat on, looking sad and lazy, and complaining of ill health. "This house," he would drawl, "is jist like a hawspital."

About a mile beyond the Ponder place stood the Hatchet Creek Baptist Church, where Missionary Baptists of the community met on the third Saturday and Sunday of each month to hear the pastor preach and possibly to hold a church conference.

The Missionary Baptist Church and its immediate vicinity may be accepted as the northern boundary of the Hatchet Creek community. But the road forked at various places and led to other homes.

At the Goza place a road branched off sharply to the east, crossed Hatchet Creek, wandered leisurely, with crook and turn, for nearly a mile over the uninhabited flatland on the left bank of the stream, and then, ascending slightly, passed the Darby place.

Dr. Darby was the community physician, and he looked the part, with his luxurious sideburns and frock coat. In the late 1870's he had attended lectures for parts of two terms at the Mobile Medical College, and though he did not graduate, he had been given a certificate to practice medicine. In the 1880's he settled in the Hatchet Creek community. His residence was an ordinary farmhouse surrounded by shade trees. In one corner of his front yard was a small frame building in which he kept his drugs, his surgical instruments, his forceps for the extraction of teeth, and other paraphernalia of his profession, for he was at once a physician and surgeon, an apothecary, and a dentist. This building was commonly called the doctor's office, but it had also the characteristics of a store. Over the counter customers could buy not only various sorts of drugs and patent medicines, but also snuff and chewing tobacco, sewing thread, and other articles commonly needed in rural households. When the doctor was away attending patients his office was usually closed, but Mrs. Darby had the key and was always willing to accommodate a customer who desired to make a purchase.

As a small boy, I could never enter the doctor's office without being painfully aware of a human skeleton reposing in an open barrel behind the counter. Once I was induced to peek into the barrel. What I saw made me shudder.

So busy was Dr. Darby with his professional duties that he had little time for farming; but he owned the farm on which his house stood, and his four sons, with the help of a hired man, usually a Negro, carried on the farming operations. Indeed, it would have been unique in the community if his sons had been allowed to loaf and get into mischief when other boys were required to labor in the fields.

A short distance east of the Darby place was Marvin's Chapel, the Methodist Church. From the elevation of the church one could, by turning one's face to the northwest,

catch a magnificent view of the valley below and the mountain range beyond, which, with an ever deepening shade of
blue, faded from sight on the distant horizon in the direction
of Horn's Valley.

The road continued eastward over the hills to Millerville
five miles farther on; but Marvin's Chapel was considered
the eastern boundary of the Hatchet Creek community.

Not far north of the Quarles place a road branched off
eastward, turned and twisted for half a mile through woodlands, and passed the residence of Elder Bennett Garrett,
Primitive Baptist pastor of Shiloh Church and my father.
Bennett Garrett divided his time and energy between preaching the Gospel according to John Calvin and growing corn
and cotton on his two hundred acre farm. Of the two activities it would be hard to say which afforded him the greater
pleasure. He dearly loved to preach and to entertain brethren
of his own faith and order in our home, and to argue Scripture
with them; but, on the other hand, he enjoyed laboring on
his farm, clearing new ground, splitting rails, and following
the mule at the plow. Since he asked nothing for his services
as pastor, and got practically nothing, he had to look to his
farm for the wherewithal to live. Our family was neither
more prosperous nor more poverty-stricken than that of the
average landowner of the community.

Within easy walking distance of our house, along the
road which now curved around a rocky hillside, was a combination grist and saw mill snugly anchored to the west bank
of Hatchet Creek. A ten foot dam across the stream impounded the water. Nearly every weekday farmers could

be seen carrying turns of corn to mill. Many of them rode on mule back with sacks of corn serving as saddles. The miller measured the corn in a cylindrical half-bushel measure and poured it into the hopper over the millstones. Then with a short handled scoop he took out his toll, roughly estimated as one-eighth, and tossed it into a stationary bin attached to the wall. Finally with a mighty tug at an upright shaft he raised the gate to the waterhouse and the upper millstone began to rotate with a low rumble which presently increased to a roar. At the level of the nether millstone a flat wooden trough, steeply inclined, conveyed the meal to a large wooden box placed at a lower level. After the miller had talked a minute or two with his customer, he descended the short flight of steps to the large wooden box, tested the fineness of the meal with his fingers, puttered with the gadget that regulated the influx of corn from the hopper, and presently began to scoop the meal into the farmer's sack. The noise and vibration of the mill, the smell of freshly ground meal, are fondly remembered by one man after the lapse of sixty years.

The sawmill was housed in an open shed forming an ell to the millhouse proper. The saw was upright instead of circular, and was effective only on the downward stroke. The log was rolled on to the carriage, carefully adjusted, and securely pinned down. When the power was turned on, a loud swish announced that the sawing process had begun. Since thirty minutes would elapse, under ordinary circumstances, before the saw ripped through the log, the sawyer could now turn his attention to other matters. If the season was summer, he was likely to seize the opportunity to snatch a little repose in the shade of a tree, or he might possibly play 'a game of marbles with the loafers who could nearly always be found at the mill. After a while a sudden acceleration in the tempo of the sawing process announced that an automatic device had stopped and reversed the carriage and that the sawyer was again needed on the job to make the necessary adjustments for ripping off another board.

The pine forest from which the sawlogs were taken covered the entire mountain range west of the valley and most of the rolling hills on the east. The trees, a yard or more in diameter, stood tall, smooth and round, without knots or limbs except at the very top. Seldom was the sapwood of the tree more than an inch in thickness; the rest was yellow heart, fine-grained, and slightly resinous. Since trees were commonly regarded as of no value until labor was applied to them, farmers felt free to cut sawlogs wherever fine trees could be found. The only consideration was the convenience of transportation. Some of the sawlogs were brought to the mill from privately owned forest land, others from the public domain in the foothills of the mountain range. For his service in converting sawlogs into lumber for the benefit of his customers, the owner of the sawmill took his toll in kind. Indeed he sometimes hitched a yoke of oxen to an enormous log cart especially constructed for the purpose, and dragged logs down from the mountainside to be sawed for his own account. But the sawmill business was not a very profitable enterprise. The market for lumber was limited and sluggish.

Above the dam was the millpond, an elongated lake, partially filled with silt. In dry weather, when the level of the water dropped, snags, stumps, brush, and tree trunks appeared above the surface, particularly on the far side of the pond across from the mill, where the impounded water had encroached upon a considerable area of the woodland. In the warm summertime turtles, both logger-heads and soft-shells, climbed upon this debris to sun themselves. From the shore small boys sometimes pelted the sunning turtles with rocks for the pleasure of seeing the startled reptiles slide from their perches into the murky water. In the summertime also, particularly on Saturday afternoons men and boys, un-hampered by any such frills as bathing suits, made use of the pond as a swimming pool. Along the wooded shores for a mile upstream fishermen could frequently be seen, silent and tranquil, waiting for the sun-perch or the wary trout to bite the hook. The miller usually kept a home-made, flat-bottomed boat, called a bateau, on the pond; but fishermen seldom used it because too much energy was required to row it upstream.

Not far below the milldam the road crossed the creek at a ford. Just above the ford an unusually long, heavy pine log, which had been carefully selected and snaked down from the mountainside, was thrown across the stream and securely anchored to a tree on each bank. The top side of the log was hewn flat with an adz; at intervals of five feet along this surface cross-pieces were let in by mortise and securely nailed down; and a fence-like hand-railing was constructed on each side, and a plank flooring laid. The result was a long, narrow bridge, about a yard wide, for the benefit of pedestrians. Children liked to stand near the middle of this bridge-like structure and, by swaying their bodies in unison, make the foot-log swing up and down.

After crossing the creek at the ford the road forked. The left prong, infrequently traveled, passed across the small upland farm and by the residence of Jasper Campbell, and continued in a northerly direction, a dim trailway through the piney woods, rendered bumpy by occasional rocks which protruded above the surface and by large tree roots which spanned its narrow width.

The right hand prong passed the residence of John Kitchings on top of the hill and, circling to the right for nearly a mile through the piney woods, came out at Ingram's mill on Little Hatchet.

This mill was much more elaborate. In addition to grinding corn into meal, it ground wheat into flour and ginned cotton; and, in addition to sawing logs into lumber with a circular saw, it boasted a workshop with power-driven machinery for the manufacture of various sorts of wooden articles needed by farmers. Anderson Ingram, who operated the shop, was an excellent carpenter and something of a cabinet-maker. Did you need a dinner table, a chest of drawers, or a pair of crutches? Anderson was just the man to make the article for you in his shop; and not infrequently he and his helper fared forth to build a new house or to repair an old one. Near the mill also was a blacksmith shop for shoeing mules and horses, sharpening plows, and performing such other services as required the forge and anvil. Moreover,

Ingram's mill had its social function: it was a convenient place for idle men and boys to meet and match their skill at marbles or croquet, or simply sit and loaf. Here the male gossip of the community was exchanged and much smutty talk indulged in.

From the mill the road crossed Little Hatchet on a bridge, ascended a hill, and passed the residence of Hezekiah Ingram, owner of the mill and father of a large family, including Anderson the carpenter. "Monk" Ingram, or "Uncle Monk," as he was affectionately called by his friends and neighbors, was taller than the average man and was decorated with a large brush of sandy whiskers. Normally he was good-natured and friendly, easy going and free from worry; but at intervals, particularly in the summertime when the Missionary Baptists were holding their revival meeting at Hatchet Creek Church, "Uncle Monk" lost his emotional balance. Though not ordained, he seized every opportunity on such occasions to preach and exhort sinners to turn from their evil ways and look to Jesus Christ for salvation, and he would emphasize the seriousness of the matter by jumping up and down, slapping his hands together, and shouting at the top of his powerful voice. For weeks after the close of a revival meeting, he might go about the daily affairs of life with the gleaming eyes of a major prophet; but with the coming of cotton-picking and fodder-pulling time, "Uncle Monk" usually cooled off and became once more his quiet, good-natured self. In addition to the mill he owned a good farm and was fairly prosperous.

From the Ingram place the road passed on to form a

junction with the Millerville road at Marvin's Chapel, with its super view of the mountain and valley to the northwest. This was the Hatchet Creek community.

CONCERNING ME

AND MY FAMILY

 I WAS THE SIXTH and last child born in our family. All I know about the circumstances attending my birth was told me, of course, by others.

For several weeks before the event, Ma, it seems, was ill-natured, gloomy, hard to live with, quite unlike her usual self. Apparently she was not pleased with the prospect of another baby in her home. A hired girl had to be brought in to do the house work and look after the children.

One night after the children were in bed asleep, they were waked up and hustled over to the Henry Harris home, about half a mile away, and put to bed there — a very unusual procedure and highly distasteful to the disturbed children. Next morning when they were allowed to return home they found Mrs. Harris there, looking very pleased. On the bed beside Ma lay the pink baby that had caused all the rumpus.

I never heard any mention of a doctor in connection with the event. The children were told that Mrs. Harris had brought the baby to their home while they slept. Until I was old enough to suspect the hoax, I felt deeply grateful to Mrs. Harris for her kindness.

Out of the haze of my earliest recollections emerge the forms and features of those who stood nearest to me, covered me with the mantle of their affections, ministered to my needs, and taught me the ways of life.

Pa, when I first became aware of his existence, was just a little short of fifty years old. He never shaved. An impression of what his face looked like may be gained by a glance at a picture of John Ruskin, the eminent English art critic and author. If Pa ever went to school anywhere I never heard him mention the experience, but somehow he had managed to master the three R's. He kept a record of his farm expenses and could calculate interest; he could draft a waive note or a mortgage for a debtor to sign; and, at leisure moments, he read the *Atlanta Constitution,* the *Gospel Messenger,* and King James's Version of the Bible. On winter evenings after supper, when the family was gathered for an hour or so around the open fire in the living room, he would sit in the chimney corner with a kerosene lamp at his elbow, reading. Ma sat in the other chimney corner, knitting. We children sat in front of the fire pretending to study our school books by the light of the blaze from resinous pine faggots; but this method of study after the fashion of Abraham Lincoln was not conducive to much learning. We children squirmed and squabbled much more than we studied.

In those days before family discipline had been reduced to a theory and consigned to such newspaper columnists as

Angelo Patri, all of us children stood in awe of Pa and gauged the extent of his dissatisfaction with our conduct by the tone of his voice. But he seldom administered punishment in anger. With an air of judicial calm he led the culprit to a lush young peachtree and slowly stripped the twigs from a sprout a yard long. Then, with many words of admonition touching the matter of wrong doing, he made the switch sing and sting while the culprit danced and wept. To none of us did the thought ever occur that corporal punishment was barbarous. We all regarded it as a just retribution for our sins and bore no malice.

I regret the passing of the old custom which required children to be respectful to their parents and other adult elders. When Pa raised his voice and called me I answered respectfully, "Sir?" Had my answer been "What?" a reprimand would have promptly followed. When addressing our adult elders, we children were taught to say "Yes, Sir," "No, Sir"; "Yes, Ma'am," "No, Ma'am"; "Mister Campbell," "Miz Campbell"; "Uncle Jim," "Aunt Mary," or "Cousin John." Less formal expressions might be "Mister Joe" or "Miss Sally." A child of ten who addressed a man or woman of fifty by his or her first name without attaching thereto some title of respect would have been regarded as an ill-mannered brat.

For some twenty years Pa was pastor of Shiloh Church, less than half a mile from our house. But, since regular services were held in that church only once a month, he was free to accept "calls" to serve as pastor of other churches as well. So far as I know he never rejected a call if he could possibly fit it into his schedule. It was not unusual to see him dress up in his best clothes on Friday afternoon or Saturday morning and ride away on horseback — he usually kept a horse for the purpose — to preach at Smyrna or some other country church within a radius of ten or twelve miles from home. On such occasions he wore a frock coat and a stiff bosom shirt with an ornate gold collar button in front, but the necktie and detachable collar were missing: the collar sawed his neck and made him uncomfortable. In his saddle bags he carried his small Testament and his hymn book for use in the pulpit, an extra pair of socks, and perhaps an extra shirt. If the weather happened to be dry and dusty, he wore a linen duster over his costume.

There is no doubt that Pa thoroughly enjoyed these preaching excursions, but there is a limit to a man's physical endurance. More than likely, on his return home, he would be suffering from a severe headache. Ma would slice pods of red pepper, add vinegar, and bind the messy mixture to his forehead. Then she would slice a pone of cornbread and toast the slices to a dark brown for him to eat. A good night's sleep usually brought complete recovery. At the end of another week Pa was ready to fare forth again, braving the discomforts of the weather and risking the danger involved in the crossing of swollen streams, to labor in the Lord's vineyard. For his services he asked no monetary compensation and received practically none.

Ma was brought up as a Methodist, but after her marriage to Pa she joined the Primitive Baptist Church. The shift in theology from the doctrine of free grace to that of election and predestination was apparently made by her without much travail of the spirit. She could hardly be called a humorist, but she had a fund of spontaneous drollery which she undoubtedly inherited from her Irish ancestors. When one was least expecting a flash of humor she would, by the turn of a phrase, throw a commonplace situation into comic relief and have everybody chuckling. Whether she attended school in her childhood, even for a few weeks, is very doubtful; but she could read fluently. Many a time as a child I have sat and listened to her read "pieces" by "Bill Arp" or "Sarge Plunkett" in the *Atlanta Constitution,* or the thrilling accounts in the same newspaper of the daring escapades of the desperado, Rube Burrow. But she never learned to write. It was with great effort that she was able to sign her name.

Ma's round of household duties began early in the morning and continued until late at night, but I cannot recall that she ever seemed hurried or harassed. She made dresses for herself and my sister Eva; she made the work clothes and knit the socks for her menfolk; she did the cooking, churning, washing, ironing, spinning, and quilting; and yet she found time to indulge in fancy needlework as a hobby. I do not recall that she ever complained of being overworked or that any of the family ever thought she was. We simply took her for granted. She was the indulgent mother who ministered to our needs and to whom we could go for help and sympathy when we were in trouble. Without her the family could not have been a going concern.

Besides parents I had brothers and sisters, nieces and nephews, and of course uncles, aunts, and cousins.

My sister Lee Anna, oldest child of the family, had been married to John Kitchings for more than a year when I was born. John had drifted into the community from a poor little farm owned by his widowed mother near Millerville, and had found employment as a hired hand. He had no property other than his personal belongings, and he never displayed any marked ambition to acquire property and get ahead in the world. In short, he became the protégé of his father-in-law. After he failed to make a living as miller at the nearby mill, he settled down as a tenant on our farm. He and Lee Anna lived across the creek less than half a mile from us.

In the Kitchings home my nieces and nephews appeared one by one until eventually there were seven of them (not counting the three that died in infancy). Since the three older nephews and I were approximately the same age, we were naturally drawn together by common interests as well as by ties of blood relationship.

During the seasons for planting, cultivating, and harvesting all boys in the community above the age of seven or eight were required by their parents to labor on the farm. The Kitchings boys and I were no exception. But Sundays were holidays, and so, too, was many a Saturday afternoon. These were the joyous intervals when a boy could call his soul his own.

At Shiloh Church there was no Sunday school because Primitive Baptists are opposed to Sunday schools. Even when preaching service was held at Shiloh on the fourth Sunday of each month, children were not encouraged to attend. Relieved thus of the necessity of receiving religious instruction, boys of Primitive Baptist families were free on Sundays to roam the fields and forests in quest of pleasure and excitement.

The Kitchings boys had a large, sturdy dog named Bulger. His ancestry was questionable, but not his ability to track down cottontails. On many a Sunday, as we roamed the pine-clad hills of the neighborhood, Bulger would suddenly flush a cottontail from its hiding place and chase it relentlessly until it found refuge in a hollow tree or hollow log or a hole in the ground. If the refuge was a hollow tree or hollow log, the quarry was as good as ours. We would cut a slender hickory withe, frazzle the small end of it and, inserting it into the hollow of the tree or log, twist it into the rabbit's fur. Careful and judicious tugging at the withe usually brought the hind legs of the distressed animal within reach of our hands.

What did we do with the rabbit after we had caught it? We knocked its life out by a blow on the head and fed the carcass to Bulger, who had a ravenous appetite for such pabulum.

One Sunday — believe it or not — Bulger flushed a white rabbit, as white as the driven snow, and chased it into a hole under a large clayroot. For two hours or more we boys delved with mattock and spade to uncover that rabbit. Suddenly and most unexpectedly it darted from its refuge and was away over the hill before Bulger's attention could be attracted to it. We never caught that one, and to this day the mystery remains unsolved. Are there such freaks in the animal world as albino hares?

On another Sunday — and fate would have it the fourth Sunday in the month — the Kitchings boys and I were joined by four Blair boys, sons of Leroy Blair. In our entourage were five or six mongrel dogs. Midday found us on the mountainside in the neighborhood of the graveyard. Suddenly the dogs flushed a cottontail which made straight for the meeting house with the pursuing pack in full cry. Pa had just reached the climax of his sermon where he was exhorting the brethren, in a sort of rhythmic chant, to "ac-centuate the positive, e-liminate the negative," when the frightened cottontail took refuge under the floor of the church and the mongrel pack stormed the works.

What happened next reached us boys only through hearsay. Chastened in spirit and fearful of what might happen to our individual hides, we fell apart into family groups and crept back home, each boy with his tail, so to speak, between his legs.

At dinner that day the glum figure of Pa at the head of the table took away my appetite for fried chicken. Before my vision floated the shadow of a peachtree covered with long sprouts. But nothing happened. A week later when we boys got together again and compared notes, we reached the conclusion that our guilt had not been discovered and that silence on our part would be the acme of wisdom.

Possibly Pa knew more about what was behind that scared rabbit than we thought he did. At a later date I was greatly enlightened by a conversation which I chanced to overhear between him and Ma.

"Do you know," Ma asked, "that Mitch was mixed up in a

fight down at the mill last Saturday and hit Jimmy Blair with a rock?"

"Yes, I know," Pa replied, "but don't let Mitch know that I know."

In our rambles over fields and forest we boys, I must admit, acquired a remarkable fund of information and mis-information about nature and woodcraft. We knew the names and characteristics of the birds, the insects, the animals, the reptiles, the plants, and the trees; we knew that the long slender snake, called the coach whip, would wrap itself around your body and whip you to death with its tail, if it ever caught you; that there was a hoop snake, though we never saw one, which took the end of its tail in its mouth and rolled rapidly along the ground like a wheel until it caught up with you and bit you, causing your death; that rattle snakes frequently "charmed" animals and people, that is, rendered them incapable of movement, so that the strike with the fangs would not miss the target. We could swim, fish, and paddle a boat; we could tie knots and chop with an ax; and with hammer and saw, auger and drawing knife, we could make our own wagons and "flying mares," as we called merry-go-rounds. But, as I look back on the days of my boyhood, I am astonished at our savage cruelty. Our hand was always raised for the destruction of every form of wild life. We fed live young birds to cats; we ground up live lizards in discarded coffee mills. Compared to such wild Indians as we were, the Boy Scout of the present day is a Little Lord Fauntleroy.

Elijah, my oldest brother, when I first became aware of

his existence, was already "a man of his own," that is to say, past twenty-one years old, but still a bachelor. He had his own horse, bridle, and saddle; he rented land from Pa "for a third and fourth"; but he continued to live with the family. About the only thing that distinguished him from the rest of us was the privilege of having a separate bedroom — a small room, ten by ten, at the west end of the front porch. In this room Lijie kept all his "things," and about his things he was as finicky as the proverbial old maid. There was no clothes closet or wardrobe or chest of drawers in the room; a heavy trunk with an oval-shaped top was used for the storage of such articles as could not be conveniently hung on nails driven into the pine-board walls. On a shelf beside one of the two windows he kept a small mirror, his shaving utensils, his two or three school books, and his tooth brush. That tooth brush could not fail to fascinate the youngest son of the family who had eyes for everything unusual. Despite parental warnings never to touch any of Lijie's things, I could not resist the temptation at times, when no one was looking, to try out the tooth brush and then replace it exactly as I had found it.

At the ripe age of twenty-eight Lijie married Sally Blair, daughter of Leroy Blair. For several months bride and bridegroom lived as members of our family, no thought ever being entertained of charging them anything for board and living space. Finally, when the season arrived for starting a new crop, they moved on to a small farm, about a mile away, which Lijie had bought a few years earlier and partially paid for.

Wilburn, my next brother, was inclined in his late teens to be restless, irresponsible, and "wild." When released from work on week ends he would saddle Jack, our tough little red mule, and go galloping about the community or to Goodwater in quest of excitement. Too often he returned home in the wee sma' hours of the morning too drunk to find his way to bed. Pa exhausted all his ingenuity in trying to correct the faults of Wilburn's character, but without success. At the age of twenty he married Frances Ingram, daughter of "Monk" Ingram, and brought his bride to our home, pending the time when he could figure out some way to make a living. After a while he rented land from our cousin, Joel Richards, and made a crop. But he remained on the Richards farm only one year. Thereafter he was the rolling stone that gathered no moss, unless perchance you call a large family of children moss.

When Warner, my youngest brother, was in his early teens, his right knee puffed up and pained him dreadfully. Dr. Darby came and pronounced the malady "white swelling." After a few days Warner could walk again, but the swelling remained and at intervals the pain returned. We all got used to seeing him "laid up with his leg" about once a month. Eventually a fistula appeared between the tendons at the back of the knee joint, which discharged puss and small bits of porous bone. He had to wear a bandage over the fistula.

During the intervals between "spells with his leg" Warner performed light labor on the farm, attended school, played ball with other boys, and even went swimming in the millpond.

One day in July, 1894, when he was nineteen years old, the fistula began to discharge a continuous trickle of blood. The disease was evidently gnawing through the wall of a blood vessel. Dr. Darby came, applied a tourniquet above the knee, and tried other devices, but failed to stop the hemorrhage. Gangrene developed in the knee. The leg would have to be amputated. A runner was sent to Goodwater for old Dr. Pope, who, be it said to his credit, recognized his limitations as a surgeon and brought along with him young Dr. Hargrove to wield the knife. Nearly a week after the onset of the hemorrhage the operation was performed in our parlor, with only a minimum of asepsis. Sympathetic neighbors, wearing their ordinary farm clothes, stood around the improvised operating table, looking on. Even I took a peek through an open window. I did not like what I saw and crept away, full of anxiety and foreboding.

For hours after the operation Warner's life trembled in the balance. Almost as white as the sheet on which he lay, he writhed on the bed and muttered nonsense, while four men stood by and tried various energetic means to restore normal warmth and circulation. Of course we know now that a blood transfusion was indicated. But what doctor in the Year of Our Lord 1894 had ever heard of a blood transfusion? Strong coffee, almost scalding in temperature, was administered; and, at long last, by the Grace of God, the crisis passed. Perhaps it was the physical stamina inherited from his pioneer ancestors that pulled him through.

Warner eventually became the owner of a valuable farm, the husband of a good woman, and a father and grandfather.

But all through the years of his adult life the ghost of his tuberculous leg, which lies buried in the graveyard at Shiloh Church, rose occasionally to haunt him. On the eve of a change in the weather a sharp pain would shoot through his sore knee, and automatically he would reach out to massage the pain away, only to find the knee gone.

My sister Eva, three years my senior, was brought up with no other thought than that she would get married at the proper age and become a housewife like her mother. To that end she was kept in the house as Ma's assistant and taught to cook, to wash and iron clothes, to sew and mend, to spin and knit, to milk the cows, and to do the various other household chores that were commonly regarded as woman's work. At the age of eighteen she met our expectations fully by marrying Bob Blair, son of Asa Blair, whom we considered to be the prize catch of the community. Bob was an intelligent, suave, and plausible young man who held forth great promise of becoming some day a prosperous citizen. He and Eva settled down to housekeeping in Talladega Valley where he rented land "for a third and fourth." But the prosperity which we expected of Bob never materialized. He never became a landowner.

Not to be omitted from the family list was Grandpap, Pa's father, who lived about a mile from us in a pioneer log house. I knew him only in his last years when he was partially paralyzed and unable to articulate well. His round, ruddy face was clean shaven except for a hedgerow of white whiskers under the chin, after the fashion of Horace Greeley. When he came for an extended visit to our home, as he occasionally did, he lived and slept in the parlor, in order to be as far away as possible from the noise and bustle of the household, and hobbled out to join the family only at meals.

When I knew him, Grandpap was irritable and crabbed, unable to endure the presence and prattle of children. In 1889, when he died at the age of eighty and was laid to rest in the graveyard at Shiloh Church, I, as a small boy of eight, watched the various phases of the burial procedure with bug-eyed wonder and delight, experiencing joy and exultation at the thought that at last Grandpap was on his way out; but joy suddenly turned into astonishment and pain when I happened to notice that Pa was weeping. In the end, I almost felt like weeping too.

Grandpap was an ordained Primitive Baptist preacher, but he only preached occasionally, when the spirit moved him. He was never pastor of a church.

A few years ago Grandpap's Bible became one of my cherished possessions. The binding is flimsy and the paper looks cheap. On the title page one reads: *"The Holy Bible containing the Old and New Testaments . . . . together with the Apochrypha . . . .* By Hervey Wilbur, A. M. New York: Published by White, Gallaher and White, No. 108 Pearl Street, 1831." The imprint of a stamping device on the corner of a fly leaf reveals that it was "Sold by Richards & Ganahl, No. 293 Broad St., Augusta, Ga." The cheapness of the edition, the date of publication, and the dealer's name stamped on the fly leaf move me to take a few known facts and family legends and, with the help of a little imagination, piece together the following story:

Grandpap was born in Lawrence District, South Carolina, on November 13, 1809. He grew up in Georgia, joined the Alcovie Baptist Church, Gwinnett County, in 1825, and was baptized by immersion in the Alcovie River. In 1840, with his wife and four small children, the youngest being my father, then three years old, he joined the migration to that part of east Alabama which had but recently been cleared for settlement by the removal of the Creek Indians. He settled down and built his log cabin in what was then the eastern part of Talladega County. Here he began to yield occasionally to an impulse which had long tormented him, to preach the Gospel, taking for his texts such familiar passages of Scripture as he happened to hold in memory. One day a colporteur came along selling a neatly bound, light weight, illustrated edition of the Holy Bible. To Grandpap he must have pointed out, as part of his sales talk, that every preacher should have a Bible and that this particular Bible had more in it than did the common run of Bibles. "See," he must have said, "here are the books of Esdras, Judith, Ecclesiasticus, Baruch, Susanna, Maccabees. I venture to say, Brother Garrett, that you never heard of them before." Whatever the sales talk was, Grandpap was persuaded and bought a Bible. What he thought about the books of the Apochrypha is not hard to surmise: he didn't ever think about them at all.

On blank pages inserted between the Apochrypha and the New Testament of Grandpap's Bible, one can read today, in a variety of faded handwritings, the family record of births, marriages, and deaths. Here is truly a human document which reduces to bare outline the story of the joys and sorrows of one of the million pioneer families that sowed the seeds of American greatness.

Grandpap was married on his birthday. He was twenty-two, his bride eighteen. The couple lived together for seventeen years and had six daughters and two sons. The older of the sons was my father, born on December 19, 1837. Less than five years after the death of his first wife Grandpap married a maiden lady of thirty-eight who quickly presented him with two children and lived to be seventy. The six daughters by the first marriage all got married, one at the age of fifteen, two at the age of sixteen, one at nineteen, one at twenty-three, and one at forty-one. The last married an elderly widower, Uncle Nat Grice, who survived the marriage less than five years.

In the summer of 1861, shortly before he was nineteen, Uncle Elijah, Pa's brother, volunteered for military service and marched away to help "repel the Northern invaders." He never came back. What happened to him is briefly told in the family record: "departed this life at Richmond, Va., on the 19th of July in the Year of Our Lord, 1862." For years Pa kept in the chest in our living room a fragment of shell extracted from Uncle Elijah's back.

Widowed by the war were three of Pa's sisters, each of whom was left with small children to support. How they kept the wolf from the door during the lean years that followed the war is not explained in the family record. When I knew them they were elderly women who lived part of the time with their married children and spent the rest of the time traipsing about the community visiting relatives and friends.

It was not unusual for Aunt Jane or Aunt Mariah to drop in on our family for a visit and prolong the visit for weeks.

Grandpa McCain, Ma's father, whom she habitually called Pappy, was married three times and was the father of seventeen children. Ma was the fourth in the first batch of seven. Since none of this family, except Ma, lived in the Hatchet Creek community, it does not seem fitting to say any more about them. But it is interesting to note that one of Ma's brothers married one of Pa's sisters and became the father of eight children. Thus I was blessed with double cousins as well as with half cousins, not to mention scores of the common variety.

WHAT WE READ

 OWING TO THE fact that Pa was a preacher, my family was perhaps a trifle more given to reading than the average of the community.

On Pa's table in our living room one could find a small Testament, a Primitive Baptist hymn book, a cheap edition of Bunyan's *Pilgrim's Progress,* a "history book," and a couple of old dilapidated volumes, seldom touched, which dealt with some such abstruse subject as Baptist doctrine.

Pa read his Testament a good deal, or at any rate held it open before his face. Occasionally on winter evenings, as we sat around the open fire, he drifted off into a snooze and let his Testament fall to the floor, creating a ripple of merriment in the family circle.

The copy of *Pilgrim's Progress* contained a dozen or more old woodcuts that impressed me greatly. Here was a picture of a fierce struggle between Christian and a huge, bat-like creature called Apollyon. Besides his great wings, Apollyon had the face and horns of an angry bull; from the unmentionable part of his body issued a cloud of smoke, presumably smelling of brimstone; in his hands he held darts which he was in the act of hurling with great force at poor Christian, who, though beaten to his knees, still managed to hold up his shield and feebly grasp his sword. How did the struggle terminate? The answer was to be found in the text, which explained that Christian at long last managed to give Apollyon such a painful thrust that he roared in defeat and frustration and vanished in a cloud of evil smelling smoke. Another picture showed the large helmet-covered head and greedy face of Giant Slay-good who hid in a cave beside the King's Highway and seized upon weak kneed pilgrims as they passed, and ate them up! When Mr. Great-Heart, armed with sword, helmet, and shield, appeared at the mouth of the cave, the giant was just getting ready to pick the bones of a captured pilgrim named Mr. Feeble-mind. There was a fierce struggle (according to the text) in which Mr. Great-Heart smote the giant, slew him, cut off his head, and rescued poor Mr. Feeble-mind.

The "history book" was an octavo volume about four inches thick, with a heavy cardboard binding which in the course of time came loose and dropped off. What made the book attractive was its wealth of pictures: rugged Norsemen armed with spears, shields, and winged helmets, rowing their long boats across the ocean and landing on our shores; savage Indians, armed with tomahawks, massacring innocent women and children, who held up their hands, pleading for mercy; British soldiers in serried ranks firing a volley point blank into a struggling, screaming mass of civilians on Boston Common; American dragoons in a battle of the Mexican

War, riding down and sabring terrorized Mexican soldiers. Other pictures showed the solemn faces of scores of soldiers and statesmen who made our country great. These faces looked out upon the reader from elaborate and ornate picture frames.

We children used to open the history book on the floor and, kneeling around it, comment on what we saw. Battle scenes were especially attractive to us. The side that appeared to be winning the battle was always claimed as "our side"; the losers were of course the "Yankees." Near the end of the book was the framed portrait of Colonel Jefferson Davis, wearing gold epaulets.

When I was about ten years old another interesting book came into our possession, though I do not remember how we acquired it. It bore some such title as *In Darkest Africa,* and was largely a compilation of adventure stories by such noted explorers as Henry M. Stanley. Confronting the reader on almost every page were pictures of lions, elephants, giraffes, rhinoceroses, hippopotamuses, crocodiles, and other dangerous beasts. There were also hunting scenes in which the intrepid white man, standing in the tall grass and wearing his pith helmet, brought down with his trusty rifle a charging lion or elephant or rhinoceros, while his black native assistants fled in terror.

But the principal source of our information about the outside world was the *Atlanta Constitution,* which, if nothing prevented, was brought to our home from the postoffice, a mile away, every Saturday afternoon.

Not long ago I had the good fortune to come across a

broken file of this once familiar paper. With a deep feeling of nostalgia I gazed upon the familiar title as upon the benign face of a long lost friend: "The Atlanta Constitution," spelled out in big ornate letters arranged in two graceful curves. Between "Atlanta" and "Constitution" one sees in the background a Southern farmhouse on pillars with a front porch and doorsteps. On the front porch are two men, one seated, the other standing, reading newspapers, presumably copies of the *Atlanta Constitution*. The doorsteps are flanked on each side by hand railings. In the front yard is a bench on which sit two beehives. Near the beehives is a woman wearing an old-fashioned sunbonnet. She is feeding a pig while several chickens hover around waiting for a chance to snatch a few grains of corn. On the right hand side, as one faces the house, is a cotton patch in which three Negroes, two men and a woman, are picking cotton. On the left hand side a white farmer wearing a broad-brimmed hat is plowing with a turning plow drawn by a horse. At the bottom of the title is a wavy ribbon bearing the words: "The Great Southern Weekly." Entwined in "The Atlanta" is a corn stalk with the shuck of the ear split open to reveal the golden grain inside. Entwined in "Constitution" is a cotton stalk with four open bolls.

The *Atlanta Constitution* of course spread its net wide to catch the interest of a great variety of readers. The front page was nearly always devoted to fiction of the short story variety and to tales of the Civil War. Other pages carried news items and editorials: pieces by Bill Arp and Sarge Plunkett; an occasional Uncle Remus story by Joel Chandler Harris; a column, part prose, part poetry, by Frank L. Stanton; the "Woman's Kingdom" under the direction of Mrs. William King; "Aunt Susie's Corner" for the children; Talmage's sermons; and advertisements.

What parts of this wide spread net caught the interest of the various members of my family?

As I remember, we youngsters seized upon the paper as soon as it arrived and looked through it for a possible Uncle Remus story, which, if found, was read by us with great avidity. Pa was chiefly interested in news items about national and state politics and about agricultural conditions in the South. Occasionally Pa read one of Talmage's sermons, only to find fault with its doctrinal exegesis. Even educated preachers, he would explain, were in most cases woefully ignorant of the Scriptures. We all enjoyed the pieces by Bill Arp and Sarge Plunkett. Ma frequently read them aloud to us youngsters, and sometimes she read them aloud when no one was there to listen. Before the paper was discarded at the end of the week, fully three-fourths of it had been read, at least superficially, by members of the family.

Bill Arp was the pen name of Charles H. Smith, a Georgia lawyer and folksy philosopher turned newspaper columnist. With homely, cracker-barrel humor and a sovereign contempt for correct spelling, he wrote about life on the farm, the rearing of children, mother love, the war and reconstruction, the people and places visited by him in his travels, and many another topic of human interest. In one of his pieces he thus characterized the war and reconstruction:

The way I see it, a big feller and a little feller, so-called, got into a fite, and they fout and fout and fout a long time, and all around everyboddy a-hollerin hans off, but kep a-hepin the big feller, till finally the little feller caved in and hollered enuf. He made a bully fite, I tell you suh. Well, what did the big feller do? Take him by the han and hep him up, and bresh the dirt offen his close? Nary time! No suh! But he kicked him atter he was down, and throwed mud on him, and drug him about, and rubbed sand in his eyes.

It goes without saying that the farmer folk of the South were Bill Arp fans. He spoke their language and expressed their sentiments; he dispensed good cheer and sound advice, and withal provoked many a good natured chuckle.

Sarge Plunkett was the pen name of Sarge Weir, a printer by trade as well as a newspaper columnist. His pieces, like those of Bill Arp, were written in what purported to be Southern dialect. They usually took the form of conversation between Old Man Plunkett who did most of the talking and a meek little character named Brown who listened and nodded approval. As a literary device to break the monotony, Old Man Plunkett was occasionally made to pause, stoop and dip his pipe in the red hot ashes, resume his easy position in his arm chair, and then proceed with the colloquy. He told war stories, indulged in reminiscences, tried to find a solution for the "nigger" problem, and descanted copiously on the sins and foibles of the times. His quaint philosophy of life was well calculated to make his readers chuckle and also, like the meek little man named Brown, to nod approval.

The column by Frank L. Stanton was designed to be clever and humorous. Though nine-tenths of the poetry consisted of rhymed jingles, not worth the space it took to print the stuff, there was an occasional stanza or series of stanzas good enough to be included in an anthology of Southern literature.

The "Woman's Kingdom" was a column devoted to a gossipy exchange of views among feminine readers, who sent letters in for publication. They exchanged views on needle work, cooking recipes, household remedies for petty maladies, and other matters of common interest. Thus Mrs. S. C. Smith of Leverett, Alabama, wrote: "Will some reader of the *Constitution* send a remedy to the Kingdom for tetter. I have had it in my hands for four years."

"Aunt Susie's Corner" was "set aside for the little friends of the *Constitution* for their entertainment and development in the art of letter-writing." Aunt Susie's picture shows a little old lady of fifty or sixty with a quaint cap on her head. She writes a long letter to her "dear children" and the children send her nicely written letters in reply.

News items of course bulked large in the *Constitution* during the eighties and nineties, but not so large as in the newspapers of the present day. Pa was interested, as I have said, in the news of national and state politics, but the rest of the family found political news rather dull and insipid. More to their taste were stories of murder, train robberies, and fleeing bandits pursued by the sheriff and his posse. Stories of this sort were full of human interest and sometimes kept us in suspense for weeks, months, and even years before we could know their outcome. Take, as examples, the stories connected with the names of Tom Woolfolk and Rube Burrow.

Tom Woolfolk, a citizen of Bibb County, Georgia, was charged with the murder of his entire family — father, step-mother, aunt, and six others. He was arrested and safely confined in the Macon jail. A long column described the gory details of the murders.

At the trial in December, 1887, Tom was convicted and sentenced to hang. But Governor John B. Gordon granted a stay of execution until the motion for a new trial could be heard and decided. In the course of time there was another sensational trial and again Tom was convicted and sentenced to death. The case was then appealed to the state supreme court which refused to grant a new trial.

On October 29, 1890, more than three years after the murders had been committed, the sheriff hanged Tom Woolfolk in the presence of six or seven thousand people who were allowed to witness the spectacle. At every stage in Tom's long and unsuccessful fight for his life, the *Constitution* gave its readers an installment of the story. It described pathetically Tom's last hours and informed its readers that he actually died of strangulation and not of a broken neck. The tone of the news articles was definitely sympathetic, and the implication was there for anyone to see that Tom probably died an innocent man.

Rube Burrow was born and raised in Lamar County, Alabama. Finding life on his father's farm pretty tame, he wandered off to Texas in 1872, when he was eighteen years old, to be a cowboy. But riding herd on the wide prairie was not exciting or lucrative enough to satisfy the cravings of this restless young immigrant from Alabama. So he became a cattle rustler. Between 1876 and 1886 it was a wise rancher who could recognize his own cows after Rube and his confederates had neatly superimposed their own brand.

In 1886 the passengers and crew of a train near Bellevue, Texas, looked into the muzzles of four rifles and surrendered their valuables. Similar robberies followed at brief intervals in Texas, Arkansas, Alabama, and Mississippi, resulting in the loss of thousands of dollars by railway and express companies. Throughout the Southeast handbills giving descriptions and offering rewards were distributed, and scores of detectives were set to work. When the law snarled too close at his heels, Rube crept back to Lamar County where he could count on his kinfolk and loyal friends to spread the mantle of silence and protection over him.

By 1889 Rube Burrow had become Public Enemy Number One, and the *Atlanta Constitution* was full of the stories of his escapades. One night he came out of a residence in response to the sheriff's summons, holding a woman before him as a shield. He was armed but he did not fire until he had backed into the woods. Then he dropped the woman, opened fire, and escaped.

In October, 1889, Rube and a confederate were surrounded near Brooksville, Blount County, Alabama, by the sheriff and a posse of forty men. The desperadoes blasted their way through the surrounding line and escaped to Sand Mountain. After a brief delay the sheriff set out in pursuit with a posse of one hundred and fifty men. Again the desperadoes blasted a gap in the surrounding line and escaped.

"In the past two years [1887-1889]," the *Constitution* informed its readers, "Rube Burrow has held up and robbed nine trains in different parts of the country, killed four men outright, wounded a half dozen more and whipped more than a hundred armed men in an open fight. His marksmanship is almost perfect. In fact, he has seldom fired at a man at a range of five hundred yards or less, without the bullet going true to the mark." He usually worked, it was explained, with only one confederate.

Shortly after the Sand Mountain affair a reporter for the *Constitution* conceived the bold design of following Rube to his lair and interviewing him for the press. Armed with a letter from Congressman Bankhead to Rube's father, Allen Burrow, the reporter, got off the train at Sulligent, Lamar County, and rode horseback the seventeen miles to the Burrow home. Allen Burrow was deeply suspicious of strangers who rode up to his front gate in the guise of book agents, lightning rod salesmen, tinware peddlers, and newspaper correspondents; but the Bankhead letter proved to be the open sesame. Allen Burrow read the Congressman's letter, relaxed, and talked at length about his notorious son. Through the grapevine, contact was made with Rube himself, who agreed to meet the reporter at a country store at Galtman, a whistle stop on the railroad, only a few miles away. The story now becomes highly dramatic, and crude pictures were drawn to illustrate the scene. Rube sat on the front porch of the store with his Winchester across his lap; the reporter sat at some distance away in a chair leant against a corner post. In response to the reporter's verbal prodding.

Rube talked freely and told the full story of his daring deeds.

This sensational interview with the notorious outlaw was published by the *Constitution* on November 12, 1889. To tease and embarrass its competitor, the *Birmingham Age-Herald*, the *Constitution* chartered a special train and sent it over to Birmingham, laden with papers. When the train arrived at its destination it was, according to the report in the *Constitution*, "utterly besieged," and for "two hours six men were kept busy" distributing papers from the platform. Newsboys yelled and fought to get papers, and before the rush was over thousands of copies had been sold. The editors and reporters of the *Age-Herald* were represented, of course, as being very properly crestfallen and red-faced from the ignominy of being "scooped" right in their own home territory.

The end of Rube Burrow came at Linden, seat of Marengo County, Alabama. The story of what happened that morning in October, 1890, is too long to tell here. Suffice it to say that when silence followed the pistol shots, Rube lay dead in the street and his antagonist, a merchant named Carter, lay severely wounded on the steps of a store.

Thereafter Rube ceased to have any news value.

But the stories of murder and banditry were not the only sensational news items in the *Constitution*. In the late 1880's that paper began to publish a series of articles about Mormon missionaries who were reported to be skulking around in Clay County, Alabama, and making converts to polygamy. In the issue of March 9, 1886, the *Constitution* said:

About 20 miles S. E. of Oxford, Alabama, along the upper part of Clay county, lies a small valley, about 12 miles in

length and from 3 to 5 miles in width, known as Shinbone
Valley. Near the center of this picturesque little valley,
upon a thickly wooded ridge and near the Ashland road,
stands a small log house, known as the Oakridge Schoolhouse
. . . . The second week of July, 1884, it was announced to the
citizens of Shinbone Valley that on the following Sunday,
Elder Kasiah of Utah would preach at Oakridge Schoolhouse.
The Elder preached according to appointment, and a few
days later he was joined by Elders Stevens and Mootry, and
the three at once went systematically to work to make converts to Mormonism.

For two years, the article goes on to say, the Elders carried on their missionary work in Shinbone Valley and vicinity
without molestation, and gathered in many sheaves for the
"Church of Latter Day Saints." But early in 1886 a committee composed of the best citizens of the community waited
on the Elders and requested them to leave. The zealous missionaries refused to leave and dared the committee to use
force. "Under the cloak of religion," concludes the article,
"these hypocrites are stirring up a feeling among the people
that sooner or later will end in bloodshed and crime."

Under date of August 28, 1888, the Mormon story continued:

News comes from Clay county, in the eastern part of the
State, of the mysterious disappearance and supposed murder
of two Mormon Elders, Davis and Weaver, who have been
preaching in that section for some time.

Mormon missionaries have been working in Clay county
for about four years and have made many converts. They
established a flourishing mission station, and have met with
but little opposition until recently. Most of the converts
have been women, and they have been hurried off to Utah.

A short time ago one of these converts wrote a letter from Salt Lake City to relatives in Clay county. The letter told a terrible story of the horrors of a life of polygamy and the outrages to which the writer and other Alabama converts had been subjected.

This aroused the people of Clay county, and the Mormon Elders were ordered to leave, but they refused to obey the order. The feeling against them among the better class of citizens was stirred to fever heat last Sunday, by a baptizing conducted by Elders Davis and Weaver. It is said that these Elders took several converts of both sexes to a mill pond and, taking them into the water in a perfectly nude condition, immersed them in the presence of about fifty people.

When this became known throughout the neighborhood, many threats against the Mormons were heard. Monday night a body of masked men went to the house where Elders Davis and Weaver were boarding and ordered them to leave the county within twenty four hours. It is said the Elders defied the crowd, and the next morning started alone for the neighborhood of Lineville to hold services at the house of a convert, and since that time they have not been seen or heard of, but it is generally believed they have been murdered and their bodies concealed by the indignant citizens of the county.

A week after the publication of this startling news item in the *Constitution*, the *Clay County Watchman*, published at Ashland, the county seat, just five miles from Lineville, came out with an editorial declaring the story of the murder of the two Mormon Elders to be entirely without foundation in fact. "As far as we can ascertain," wrote the editor, "no Mormon elders have been in this section for at least four years, and so far as their 'flourishing mission' is concerned, we failed to find any one with the slightest knowledge of it."

Under date of March 26, 1889, the *Constitution* carried a spread of more than three columns on Mormon activities in the South. Here is an extract from it:

About two hundred Elders are now at work in the South and nearly one hundred of them are in Alabama. They are operating in about a dozen counties, but their stronghold is in Clay county, where their church is located. From this point they work the adjoining counties of Cleburne, Randolph, and Talladega.

It must have been around the year 1889, when I was eight years old, that two strangers traveling on foot appeared at our front gate one day and called, "Hello!" Pa went out to see what they wanted, and I trailed along after him to satisfy my curiosity. They explained that they were ministers of the Gospel representing the "Church of Jesus Christ of Latter Day Saints" and that they wanted to use the community schoolhouse for religious services on a certain date. "The Church of Jesus Christ" sounded familiar to Pa, but "Latter Day Saints" did not click with him, and he asked for further enlightenment. In response the strangers handed him a printed sheet of paper, about four by six inches in size, which, they explained, contained their articles of faith. Since Pa could not read well without his glasses, he went back into the house to get them.

As soon as Pa turned to go, the strangers sat down to rest at the base of a nearby shade tree. From my stance just inside the gate I gazed at them in silent wonder. They were dressed pretty much alike — black hats and long black coats;

even their beards were alike. I would have been willing to admit that they looked like preachers, but I had never before seen preachers look so weary and travel stained.

In a few minutes Pa reappeared, walking slowly from the door steps to the gate, reading the printed sheet of paper. Suddenly his footsteps quickened and his eyes flashed with anger. He had come to the name Joseph Smith at the bottom of the sheet, and that name clicked with him in a big way.

"Yes," he said in a pugnacious tone, "you are Mormons! You want to destroy our families and enslave our women."

"No! No!" protested the strangers, springing to their feet. "We do not practice polygamy."

"Yes, you do!" Pa insisted, and the altercation became loud and animated. All three men talked at once, their beards wagging angrily.

"Be on your way," Pa kept saying. "Git off my property."

The last I saw of the weary, footsore strangers, they were trudging down the road in the direction of the footlog that crossed the creek.

In the absence of telephones, communication was slow in the community; but in a couple of days the exciting news got around that Mormons were in our midst. A watch was kept on the schoolhouse and threats were made that, if any Mormon showed up there to hold religious services, he would be promptly tarred and feathered. No Mormon ever showed up.

Whatever became of the two Mormon Elders I never knew, nor what their names were; but I am sure that they were not murdered in our community or even tarred and feathered. They evidently decided that we were hard nuts to crack and wandered on to another community in search of nuts with softer shells.

Prize fighters were just beginning to attract public attention around 1890. The *Constitution* called them pugilists, an unusual word, in pronouncing which we habitually gave the "g" a hard sound as in Gilson. The pugilist that won my undivided allegiance was John L. Sullivan, a ponderous Irishman with a walrus mustache, who boasted that he was the champion of the world; but he admitted that Jim Corbett and Jake Kilrain would have to be shown that he was the champion. The fight between him and Corbett took place at New Orleans in September, 1892. The *Constitution* devoted an entire page to it. There were pictures showing the combatants shaking hands in the arena, the combatants exchanging blows, and finally the bulky form of John L. on the floor, unable to rise. Scientific pugilism, it was explained to us, had prevailed over brute force. However that may have been, I still entertained great personal affection for the big, boastful Irishman, and hoped that some day he would stage a comeback, which he never did. From that sad day in September, 1892, until the present, I have never been much interested in prize fights.

In addition to the *Constitution,* Pa usually subscribed for the *Clay County Advance,* published weekly at Ashland, and for *Farm and Fireside,* published biweekly at Springfield, Ohio. The *Advance* was largely a one-man paper, reflecting the views and opinions of the editor and owner and publishing only such news and opinions as the editor deemed interesting and appropriate. In its columns the reader could find news and discussions of state and county politics and of the activities of the Farmers' Alliance. From communities in various parts of the county local reporters each week sent in personal items which the editor was usually glad to get to serve as space fillers. Only in election years were county newspapers eagerly read, and then only by adults.

Farm and Fireside could hardly be called a newspaper. Its main purpose was to stimulate farmers to improve their methods of tillage.

What we read was not conducive to much culture or sound learning, but we read enough to keep in practice and to have a fair knowledge of what was going on around us. In 1892, for instance, when the news reached us that Grover Cleveland was elected, I knew, although I was only eleven years old at the time, that our country was again safe in the keeping of the Democratic party, and I rejoiced greatly.

ANIMAL HUSBANDRY

or WHAT YOU WILL

 AS A GENERAL RULE, farmers of the Hatchet Creek community kept cattle, sheep, goats, and hogs, which had access during most of the year to the free range, that is, to the wide extent of woodlands outside the cultivated areas. To distinguish his animals from those of his neighbors, a farmer devised some sort of distinctive marking. My father's mark was a smooth crop off the tip of the right ear. One of our neighbors had a much more elaborate marking: a crop and a slit and an underbit in both ears. When the operation was finished, the poor animal had little left of its auricular appendages. Nearly every winter forest fires, deliberately set, swept over the free range, destroying the underbrush and improving the next summer's pasturage. Since the leaves and pine needles were not thick on the ground, such fires were not injurious to the tall trees.

A farmer's cattle seldom wandered far away on the range. Usually his small herd stayed together, following in the wake of the old milk cow that wore the bell and returning home with her at night. In the late fall, when the range ceased to offer sufficient pasturage, the herd was turned into the farmer's harvested cornfield in the fertile bottomlands to vegetate until spring, without much reference to the corn crib or the fodder loft. The milk cows, however, were brought in at night from this improvised pasture, placed in the cow pen, and fed night and morning a mixture of corn meal and raw cotton seed. The latter ingredient had little nutritive value; it may even have contained properties injurious to the animal; but it served quite adequately as a filler. Needless to say, the yield of milk per day was not large — less than a gallon for each cow.

In the late fall also the flocks of sheep and goats, which had wandered away during the summer months and become half wild on the range, returned to their respective owners for salt and winter feeding, bringing their unmarked younglings with them. Their feed during the winter was also corn meal and cotton seed; but, being more finicky about their eating than were the milk cows, they licked up the meal and usually left the cotton seed in the trough. In April or May, before the sheep fell into the habit of staying away over night and losing themselves again on the range, they were rounded up and sheared. The shearing was done by hand with large shears which could be bought on the market or borrowed from a neighbor, and the fleece was afterwards cleansed by a thorough washing with a liberal application of soap.

For some reason farmers of the community had an aver-

sion to eating mutton; but they considered goatmeat a delicacy, especially in the summertime when fresh pork was not
readily available. When a farmer was expecting numerous
guests, as, for instance, during the district meeting at the
Primitive Baptist Church in August, or the revival meeting
at one of the other two churches, or during any other gathering which drew visitors from a distance, he might slaughter
one of his yearling goats to supplement his supply of fried
chicken.

At the dinner table, after the blessing was asked, the host
would proudly pass a huge platter of fresh meat to his guests
with the invitation: "Have some of the kid, brethren." So
far as the records disclose, no Baptist brother, nor Methodist
either, ever declined to take a generous helping.

The hide of the slaughtered goat was deprived of its hair
by some sort of evil-smelling process and tanned by the
farmer himself, or by one of his neighbors skilled in the
art, for use as whang leather. If the tanning was properly
done, the product was soft and pliant. Thin strips, sometimes
more than two feet long, could be sliced off the leather by
means of the sharp blade of a pocket knife and used as twine
for the repair of harness or as laces for heavy shoes. "Get the
whang leather" was a frequent request in farmers' homes
when a tough and durable ligament was needed for any
purpose.

Hogs, too, were turned out on the range to feed on
acorns and other mast, and to plow the soft humus with their
snouts in quest of succulent roots; but hogs, like squirrels
and raccoons, being able to live indefinitely in the forest,

were subject to wanderlust and to forgetfulness of the loved
ones back home. A farmer, in consequence, encouraged his
hogs, by giving them access to a little food now and then,
to feel that they had a stake in the old home place. At nightfall they were usually admitted to the enclosure called the
lot, where the mules and horses were fed, and to the cow
pen; they picked up stray grains of corn here and there and
rooted freely in the manure; occasionally they were regaled
with a few nubbins casually tossed to them. No hog was
expected to grow fat on such meager fare; but, what with
rooting in the nearby woods, the animal was expected to
subsist with a certain degree of felicity until the time came
for it to be put in a pen and fattened for the slaughter.

In the spring a farmer who had a good sized family to feed
selected three or four of his most promising shoats for fat-
tening. The pen in which they were confined was built in
a shady spot on firm ground, in a corner of the lot, and was
provided with a deep, solid trough. Into the trough was
dumped, at convenient times during the day, the garbage
from the kitchen — sour buttermilk, stale biscuits and pieces
of cornbread, and other left-overs from the table, and, for
good measure, the used dishwater also. The imprisoned
shoats welcomed the approach of the slop bucket from the
kitchen with grunts and squeals of delight and could not wait
for all the contents to be poured into the trough before they
began to feast greedily. Into the pig pen was also dumped
at odd times the waste from the orchard, the vegetable garden,
and the melon patch.

Not much can be said in praise of the sanitary condition

of the pig pen. The odor that arose and the flies that swarmed were two sufficient reasons for locating the pen at some distance from the dwelling house.

In the fall, corn was added to the menu of the penned up shoats — as much corn as they could eat. They now waxed in avoirdupois until they came to weigh as much as two hundred pounds apiece. The proud farmer would sometimes invite casual passers-by to pause for a moment and admire them.

Hog killing time came on a frosty morning in late December or early January. The gory details of the process need not be described; but rendering lard and preparing chitlings may be mentioned as an interesting part of the saturnalia.

After the warm, liquid lard was strained through a thin cotton cloth the residue was a crisp brown mass of cracklings, which were highly prized as shortening for cornbread. This "shortening bread," as it was called, was a rather heavy diet, but it was toothsome, and its fame has been celebrated in at least one of our Southern folksongs.

The preparation of chitlings was a long drawn-out process, but the end justified the means. Boiled until thoroughly cooked and tenderized, and then fried in batter, chitlings were simply out of this world. As a small boy I could eat chitlings until my sides stuck out.

For several days after a hog killing we always had an abundance of fresh meat which, in the absence of refrigeration, had to be eaten without too much delay — liver, lights, sweetbreads, chitlings, pig's brains, pig's feet, spare ribs and backbone, and what have you; but an attempt was made to preserve the rest of the porcine carcass for future consumption. Souse meat would keep for a considerable time, and sausage would keep even longer. The sausage was highly flavored with sage and pepper, wrapped in thin cotton cloth or stuffed into a carefully cleansed and prepared intestine, and hung in the smokehouse to dry. The hams, shoulders, and middlings were given a light sprinkling of salt and presently suspended from horizontal poles in the smokehouse over a smoldering fire of corn cobs and green hickory logs. If the curing process was carried out properly, the resulting bacon was covered with a greenish crust, impervious, at least in theory, to the encroachment of insects. Fortunate, however, was the farmer who did not find his bacon in the summertime infested with skippers, that is, frisky, white worms, about half an inch long, which burrowed into fatty areas and, when disturbed, twisted themselves into knots and skipped like tiny grasshoppers. Too often for appetite's sake dead skippers were found at the bottom of the gravy bowl.

All home-processed pork was called bacon. Salt pork was a highfalutin expression seldom heard in the community, and then only in connection with the purchase of side-meat, or fat-back, on the market at Goodwater or Talladega.

To protect their crops from roving domestic animals, farmers were obliged to fence in their cultivated areas. This they did by felling pine trees and splitting them into rails, with which they built zigzag fences — miles of zigzag fences. Fortunately rails split from resinous pine lasted almost indefinitely, unless perchance a forest fire crept up behind the farmer's back and reduced his fence to ashes.

The free range has now of course passed into the penumbra of half forgotten things, and its passing is not to be regretted. Under that system of husbandry there was no possibility of careful breeding of domestic animals or of care for their health. Cows were afflicted with hollow horn and hollow tail, and had to have holes bored in their horns and slits made in their tails. Grubs, popularly called "wolves," appeared in little pockets just beneath the skin on the backs of undernourished cattle. I have seen the hinder parts of cows and calves literally covered with gorged ticks of enormous size. In the summertime all the animals carried ticks and redbugs, even the chickens. Small boys who wandered about in the woods hunting blueberries or merely breathing the ozone of the pines came home covered with these parasites. Picnickers on the Glorious Fourth scratched ticks and redbugs while they listened to the spread eagle oratory.

Good riddance, then, to the free range!

For draft animals farmers of the community used mules, horses, and sometimes oxen.

The mule is, by common report, a stubborn animal; but he can hardly be called stupid. By some sort of intuitive process he understands that everybody is laughing at him because of his long ears and other asinine characteristics; but for all that, he is not downhearted or afflicted with an inferority complex. He reasons that, since nobody loves him, it is up to him to fend for himself; and, if he should be so fortunate on occasion as to outsmart his human counterpart, he may even raise his voice in a derisive hee-haw. Unless his stable door is securely locked at night he will think it clever to raise the latch or remove the peg with his muscular upper lip and let himself out. A similar operation on the crib door will give him access to the ears of corn inside. But rest assured, he will never eat enough to injure his health. Rather than fall into the lap of that error, he will much prefer to pick up the ears of corn one by one and scatter them all over the lot, to the discomfiture and harassment of his master. As a faithful slave, he will serve for years just for the fleeting pleasure of giving his master one swift kick at the first opportune moment.

Nevertheless, in my day and generation, the mule was commonly regarded as the best fitted of all the domestic animals for farm work. He ate much less than a horse did; he could draw the plow all day long at a uniform, plodding pace, without the loss of much perspiration. If slashed with the plow line by an irate plowman, or sworn at vociferously, he did not lose his emotional balance, dance about, and crush the life out of all the small plants within reach of his feet, as a horse would do under such circumstances. Instead, he took his beating philosophically and dismissed the untoward incident from his mind as soon as possible.

A farmer who operated three plows, which was about the average number, would normally keep a matched pair of mules to draw the wagon about the farm or to market, and a horse for the buggy on Sundays or other special occasions. A mule of course might be pressed into service as a buggy horse, and frequently was, but riding in a buggy behind a stolid mule was not regarded as exactly *comme il faut* by the *élite* of Hatchet Creek society. If a farmer had much heavy hauling to do, he usually kept a yoke of oxen for the purpose. In our community, however, an ox drawing a plow was an unusual spectacle which always excited the mirth of passers-by.

The normal family had two or three saddles hanging in the gear house for horseback riding. On Sunday afternoons, which was the normal time for courting, the grown sons of the family would saddle horses and mules and fare forth in quest of romantic adventures. Given time, the mule could always deliver its rider at the appointed place, but there was never anything about the manner of delivery to remind one of the days when knighthood was in flower. Even when bearing an impatient lover on its back, the stubborn animal took great pains to conserve its health and energies.

Perhaps one family out of five possessed a side saddle for the benefit of the womenfolk. For the convenience of feminine riders, a solid mounting block, consisting of two or three steps, was not an unusual sight just outside the front gate of a well appointed home. In ascending and descending the block, the lady was very careful not to expose her pretty ankles.

In connection with animal husbandry, the fact should be recognized by all concerned that the Lord has endowed all animals with the sex impulse. Unless that impulse is eliminated, except in the case of those animals selected to propagate the species, the consequences, from the farmer's point of view, are unsatisfactory. Nowadays a veterinarian is called in to modify what the Lord hath done. But in the Hatchet Creek community there was no educated and scientifically trained veterinarian. So the farmer himself took out his rusty pocket knife, whetted the blade on the gritty sole of his shoe, and transformed male pigs and male calves into eunuchs without benefit of education or science; and with the same instrument, with perhaps a little more caution, he transformed his female pigs into sexless creatures. If any of the patients ever died from the operation, the matter has escaped my memory.

Only one or two farmers in the community had the courage and acquired skill to alter male horses or male mules. When an operation of this sort was to be performed, one of the animal's front legs was bent up at the knee and bound in that position. With only three legs to walk on, the poor animal was led around in a wide circle by a halter and flailed occasionally to keep it moving, until at length it dropped to the ground from sheer exhaustion. Quickly now its four feet were securely bound together and the sharp knife applied. No anesthetic was used. To stop hemorrhage and prevent infection, the fresh wound was seared with a hot iron. If the patient survived, we all rejoiced; if the patient died — well, better luck next time. As a matter of fact, nearly all the patients survived.

Besides domestic animals, all farmers kept chickens and geese, and some kept a few ducks, turkeys, and guineas as well. But no special care was ever taken of any of them. At night the fowl roosted here and there about the premises — on low branches of fruit trees, in fence corners, in the tool-shed, according to their fancy. According to their fancy also, hens made their nests in the fodder loft, in the corn crib, in the feed trough of the stable, in the corner of the fence, or under the floor of the dwelling house. It was not hard for a housewife to locate a nest, for a hen can not refrain from a fit of loud cackling immediately after having laid an egg. When a hen showed a determination to set, she was usually treated with a good deal of deference and supplied with a dozen or more eggs, so that her longing for motherhood could be gratified in a big way. For a few days after the blessed event, mother and chicks were kept in a coop and fed corn-meal dough, until the chicks were strong enough to follow the clucking hen about the yard and the adjacent fields in quest of juicy bugs and other interesting bits of nourishment. In the late afternoon of each day the housewife called all of her adult and adolescent fowl (except the geese) to a rendezvous in the back yard — hens, roosters, friers, turkeys, and guineas — for a banquet of cornmeal dough which she scattered with a lavish hand from her capacious dishpan. By stooping over stealthily, while the greedy fowl were eating near her feet, she could seize an adolescent rooster by the leg and hold him for future reference. Breakfast was the favorite time for eating fried chicken.

Every summer chicken peddlers, driving light wagons equipped with wire coops and loaded with boxes of merchandise, made the rounds of the community, offering to exchange merchandise for chickens and eggs. A peddler's best customers were the womenfolk, who could not resist temptation when he held up bright calico or shiny cooking utensils for exchange. Very obligingly he offered to catch the chickens himself, and he always proved himself very adept at the job. From a convenient rack in his wagon he would take a long, heavy, straight wire with a sharp crook at one end. With this instrument he could pick up friers about the yard and lot faster than a small boy could catch spot-tails and sun-perch at the millpond.

A very great handicap in raising chickens was the depredation of hawks and varmints. The hawk that did the most damage was the one we called the "blue darter" — not a large bird but swift on the wing. It would take its stance on the bare limb of a tall tree, preferably a dead pine, overlooking the farmyard and wait for its opportunity. When it spotted a brood of chicks following a mother hen, it came in like a miniature dive bomber and carried away a chick, amid the loud squawks and cackling of all the fowl in the farmyard. The irate housewife might run out and cry "Shoo!" but to no avail. The blue darter came back on other days when it was again hungry, and there were many blue darters.

To detect the presence of hawks before any damage was done and to chase them away, black martens were often induced to come and form a nesting colony near the farmyard. The inducement was a tall, slender pole made from a sapling with wide spreading branches, to which eight or ten gourd birdhouses were attached. Once having discovered the pole and availed themselves of its accommodations, the martens would return to it year after year in the springtime, raise their young, and depart in the late summer. During the nesting season, they darted in and out of their gourd houses, chattered noisily, and kept an anxious eye out for hawks. When a hawk was discovered they set up a cry of alarm,

which alerted the whole farmyard, and darted out to attack
the marauder and chase him away with their sharp beaks.
Thus many a chick escaped a sudden and horrible death, and
the heart of many a housewife was made glad, by the presence
of black martens on the premises.

The most troublesome varmints were minks and 'possums.

The mink came in from the swamplands at night and at-
tacked grown chickens. It would creep up on a mother hen
brooding over her chicks in the fence corner and bite the
back of her neck, or it would attack a chicken roosting on
the fence top. There was always a squawk from the victim
and, if the farmer and his dog moved quickly, they could
scare the varmint away before it had done much damage.
Otherwise, it would kill several chickens and gnaw their
heads off. As soon as the dog appeared on the scene of the
crime, the night prowler darted away to its accustomed
haunts and easily lost itself in the maze of ditches and
streams. No successful trap was ever devised by farmers of
the community for catching minks. Steel traps set where
minks were supposed to run usually caught dogs and cats,
if indeed they caught anything at all.

A hungry 'possum, when it came prowling about a farmyard at night, was attracted to the young chickens nestling
under the wing of the mother hen in the fence corner. The
squawking of the disturbed hen would quickly bring the dog
to the scene; and Mr. Possum, not being able to run fast
enough to make good his escape, was usually caught *in
flagrante delicto* and promptly dispatched there and then
without due process of law. Although, according to common

report, Southern Negroes had great relish for baked 'possum and sweet potatoes, Southern white people seldom indulged in that delicacy, even during the fat persimmon season.

For want of proper care, turkeys in the Hatchet Creek community did not thrive. The young ones were delicate, and easily succumbed to the chill of wet weather and to the fatigue engendered by their efforts to follow their high-stepping mothers over the fields in pursuit of grasshoppers. It was the exceptional housewife who had more than half a dozen turkeys, including the old gobbler which strutted about the farmyard, frightening small children. Under the circumstances, then, roast turkey could seldom be served at Thanksgiving or at any other time during the year, and cranberry sauce was not even heard of.

Guineas were kept mostly for the sake of their exotic beauty and for the pleasure of listening to their cheerful voices as they seemed to say "pot-rack, pot-rack." No one ever ate a guinea, and guinea eggs were not in favor.

As for geese, in the days of feather beds, geese were a necessity. Every housewife had a large flock of them, which, thanks to the hardy nature of the fowl, could thrive and multiply without much care or attention on her part. Except during the winter months, when a few handfuls of corn had to be tossed to them occasionally, geese were able to fend for themselves. In the spring they ate grass and tender shoots wherever such pabulum could be found. They waddled around outside the rail fences looking for an opening through which they could squeeze their bodies into a field of young corn. Once in a field, they could wreak great havoc in a very short time. When a farmer came upon a flock feeding on his young crops, he usually lost his piety and fell from grace. If the predatory fowl happened to belong to a neighbor, the matter might become serious. I knew two brothers-in-law who came to blows over the depredations of a flock of geese.

Spring is the mating season for geese. The female of the species makes her nest in a remote fence corner or thicket. When she has completed the process of laying an egg, she does a very effective job of covering her nest with leaves and such other rubbish as may be lying around. Then she emerges from her hiding place and calls to her mate: "O Abraham!" and the gander, from his stance not far away, answers: "Here I am!"

One day my brother Warner, then about twelve years old. came upon a setting goose in a thicket. She extended her long neck and hissed a dire warning; but, paying no heed, he poked her with a long stick in the hope of discovering how many eggs she had under her. Before he had time to say "Jack Robinson," the goose was upon him, grasping the skin of his tummy with her beak and beating him vigorously with the butts of her wings. When the battle was over, she called lustily for Abraham and the gander answered her, but Warner did not tarry to hear what they had to say to each other. The bruised spot on his tummy, which presently turned black, was no laughing matter. He had learned a valuable lesson from the female of the species.

Goose feathers were picked in the late spring, when the geese began to show a tendency to shed their winter habiliments and put on fresh ones. The process began with the rounding up of the long-necked fowl and the enclosing of them in the lot, where they could be easily caught. Then a summons was sent to the housewife who came with a chair in one hand and a basket in the other. She seated herself in the chair and the children of the household, full of zest and excitement, brought the squawking, flapping geese to her one by one. She took the goose by the neck, flopped it over on its back in her lap, and plucked the soft feathers from its underside and elsewhere, and placed the feathers in the basket. When the goose was released it still had the long, hard feathers of its tail and wings and the tiny feathers on its neck, but the rest of its body was now covered only with down. How much pain was inflicted by the plucking is only a matter of conjecture. When the goose was released, it seemed to be considerably flustered, but as soon as it had reached a safe distance it usually flapped its wings and gave vent to what sounded like a shout of defiance to its tormentors.

Before being put to use, the feathers were "cured," that is, thoroughly aired and dried in the sun.

Nowadays feather mattresses are hard to come by and are sometimes decried by people who do not have them as injurious to the health; but sixty years ago they were to be found in all the farmhouses of the South, and they were a great boon to people who had to sleep in unheated bedrooms.

Other than feathers, geese contributed nothing to the economy of the Hatchet Creek community. No one ever ate a goose. Mercy, no! Perhaps a fat duck now and then, but a goose, never!

HOW WE MADE A LIVING

 WHEN THE FIRST SIGNS of spring appeared in late February or early March, something stimulated farmers to shake off the lethargy of winter and gird themselves for another tussle with Mother Earth. This urge to be up and doing did not originate in a stern sense of duty but seemed to spring from an effervescence in the blood. Adolescent boys and girls lost interest in their books and dropped out of school; young men and old men furbished up their farm tools and fared forth into the fields; up and down the valley in the early mornings could be heard the high-keyed and sometimes rhythmical hallooing of young men and boys: "Ho-hee-hee, ho-hee-hee, ho-hee-ho-hee-ho-hee-hee!" It was spring and time to start the crops.

The first task of the farmer was to prepare his land for the spring plowing. With ax, hoe, and brier hook, he proceeded to remove the bushes and briers from fence corners and ditch banks; dry cornstalks from the last year's crop were chopped down with hoes, piled up, and burned; dry grass on the bottomlands was burned off. If any new ground had been cleared during the winter months, the brush heaps were now burned and perhaps a day was set for a log-rolling, when neighbors would be invited in to help pile the heavy logs for burning.

When the farmer was ready to plow, he led his mule from the stable, clamped a shuck collar on its neck, and with a deft movement acquired from long practice threw over its back the simple gear, which consisted of hames, trace chains, canvas backband, and rope lines. The light plow-stock was made of wood, but to the wooden beam was firmly bolted a wrought iron "foot," or share-beam, to which the detachable plowshare was fastened by a heel bolt. To the singletree, which was linked by a lap ring to the clevis at the front end of the wooden beam, the trace chains were hooked. When the mule was properly hitched up, the plow-man, looping the rope lines loosely about his wrists and grasp-ing the handles of the plowstock, made a loud clucking sound with his tongue and cheek, which the mule was supposed to interpret as a command to get going. If the clucking sound was ignored by the animal, which was likely to be the case, the plowman slapped its side with a rope line and uttered an imperative "Get up!"

The spring plowing was done with moldboards which turned the soil to the right, leaving a clean furrow. The area to be plowed was laid off in rectangular "lands." Around each land, counter-clockwise, mule and plowman plodded until the last furrow was run. The mule learned to walk on the unplowed soil close beside the furrow. If it strayed too far to the left, the plowman said "gee"; if too far to the right, he said "haw." Mules soon learned the meaning of "gee" and "haw" and moved back into place at the word of command.

Stumps, with their wide-spreading roots, were the bane of the plowman, especially if the plowman happened to be an adolescent boy. When the point of the plow struck a stump, the handles of the plowstock would fly up with a quick jerk and drop back with a vigorous punch. As they went up they would likely catch the plowman under the chin and snap his teeth together, and as they came down they rarely failed to give him a dig in the stomach which would knock the last prop from under his tottering piety. When the plow came to a root that was weak and yielding enough to serve its impious purpose, it would creep cautiously under the thing, stretching it to its utmost tension, till the mule slackened speed. Then the plowman would slash the mule with the plowline, the mule would make an extra surge, the root would snap, the plow would slip through the rent, and both ends of the broken root would come back on defenseless shins with force enough to bark them from ankles to knees.

Each farmer had his own harrow, which was a heavy, wooden affair, in the form of a V, equipped with iron spikes for pulverizing the clods. Drawn by two mules, or preferably by a yoke of oxen, the clumsy contrivance went rolling and pitching over the plowed soil like a ship in distress at sea. So heavy was the draft on the shoulders of the animals and so ineffective was the operation of the machine that harrowing was sometimes dispensed with and the planting process undertaken without benefit of soil pulverization.

The season for planting corn was May and early June. The rows were from four to five feet apart and the hills in each row a yard apart. A shovel plow, so named from its shape, was used to lay off the rows. In areas which lacked fertility manure was applied. The manure was taken from the stables and the cow pen, loaded on to a wagon, and drawn into the field where it was distributed by hand. The work was repulsive and exhausting, requiring strong stomachs and muscular backs. Three or four men, carrying heavy bags of manure swung over their shoulders by straps, walked beside the furrows and dropped large handfuls at three foot intervals. After a field had been manured, small boys came along carrying pails of carefully selected seed corn and dropped two or three grains beside each handful of manure. A plowman followed the boys and lightly covered the seed with soil.

Corn was usually cultivated until the stalks were as high as the plowman's shoulders. Hoes were applied at least twice during the growing season to thin out the plants and remove grass and weeds from the rows, and the "middles" were plowed out at least three times with scrapes. Scrapes varied in lateral spread from twelve to twenty-four inches, and in width of wing from two to three inches. The wings were set at an angle of about thirty degrees to the surface of the ground and were dragged under the soil to the depth of about an inch and kept in place by a long, slender plow called a scooter which, like the scrape, was bolted to the share-beam. Three furrows with a scrape between two rows of corn sufficed to cleanse the middle of weeds and grass and pulverize the top soil. By mid-July the corn crop was laid by, that is to say, no longer cultivated.

Corn was most productive when planted in the alluvial soil of bottomlands; cotton, in the thin soil of uplands.

Cotton rows were not so wide apart as those of corn, and more preparation was needed before the seed was planted. After the cotton rows had been laid off (in conformity with the contour of the hillsides to discourage erosion), commercial fertilizer had to be applied to insure a good crop. This commodity, popularly called guano irrespective of its ingredients, was purchased from merchants in Goodwater or Talladega. It came in two hundred pound bags, and some kinds of it smelled to high heaven. For its distribution a guano strower was needed. This instrument was a light tin tube, or pipe, about four feet long and about two inches in diameter, with a funnel at one end. The operator walked beside the furrow, with a small bag of guano strapped to his shoulder, and by means of the strower deposited a thin ribbon of the fertilizer at the bottom of the furrow. On windy days the operation was difficult and the task hateful. Guano blew into the operator's face and adhered to his moist lips; its evil odor clung to his clothing. Until he had bathed thoroughly and put on clean clothes, he could be detected at a considerable distance by the sense of smell.

Thrice around the fertilized furrow a moldboard was run, throwing up a "bed." On top of the bed the cotton seed was planted.

Progressive farmers provided themselves with cotton seed planters.

The planter was a clumsy contraption which consisted of a plowstock, a wheel, a side arm, a hopper, and a drag mounted on two strips of steel. The side arm worked a ratchet inside the hopper which poured a roll of seed in a continuous wasteful stream, to be lightly covered by the drag which followed. The contraption was drawn along on top of the bed by a mule and held in place by a plowman who walked behind grasping the plowhandles.

Farmers who were either too conservative or too poverty-stricken to buy planters devoted more time and labor to the planting process.

Cotton seeds coming from the gin are covered with fragments of lint, which cause them to cling together. To paste the lint to the seeds and thus reduce them to the consistency of dry peas, farmers used ashes from the ash hopper in the back yard. Cotton seed, ashes, and water were thoroughly mixed by stirring them with a rake or hoe and the mixture was then spread out to dry. Thus processed, the seeds could be strown along in the shallow furrow on top of the bed by means of the guano strower, and afterwards lightly covered by means of a V-shaped drag bolted to the share-beam of the plowstock.

Young cotton plants turn black and die when the temperature drops below fifty degrees. Early May, therefore, after the chilly nights had subsided, was the time for planting. If the rainfall was adequate, late May or early June was the time for "chopping."

Cotton chopping time was the busiest season of the year, when all available hands, young and old, were pressed into service. Some of the family, usually the adult members, had to turn their attention to planting the corn, a task which could not be postponed. The rest of the family, usually the children, with possibly an experienced hand to guide and instruct them, had to chop the cotton.

The chopping was done with hoes. With a scraping movement across the row, the manipulator of the hoe thinned out the plants, leaving healthy ones at eighteen inch intervals, and removed all weeds and grass. It was a tedious task, trying to the muscles, to the patience, and even to the souls of those who wielded the hoes. I well remember those long, hot days. After lazily agitating the hoe for a few minutes, I would lean on the handle, prop a bare foot against the knee of the opposite leg, and gaze at the slow moving sun. I learned to estimate the lapse of time with a fair degree of accuracy by measuring with my eye the distance between the sun and the horizon. When the dinner horn blew at noon, children and adults responded with loud shouts, and it was not at all uncommon for mules also to bray in response. For an hour now there was respite from toil, while men, children, and mules ate their dinners and relaxed. At one o'clock the work was resumed and continued until the sun went down.

Cotton was cultivated until the last days of July, when incipient bolls which farmers called "squares," although they were in reality triangular in shape, appeared on the plants, followed by blossoms. When squares appeared the cotton was laid by.

Secondary crops were wheat, oats, and sorghum. Wheat

was sowed in the fall, oats in the spring; both were reaped
in June and July. The reaping was done by cradle. The
cradler was followed by another person who picked up the
grain and bound it into bundles. Until the farmer could find
a convenient time to haul the grain to the barn, the bundles
were brought together in batches of twelve and "shocked"
in the field; that is, ten bundles, packed together as closely
as possible, were stood up on their butt ends and capped
with the other two bundles spread out fan-wise to form a
roof. These shocks of golden grain sometimes stood in the
field for weeks before they were removed.

In the course of time an itinerant thrash, accompanied by
a wood-burning engine, rolled into the farmer's lot. Both
the thrash and the engine, being very heavy, were usually
drawn by yokes of oxen. When on the road the engine's
smoke stack, topped by a bulky device for the discourage-
ment of flying sparks, lay horizontally along the full length
of the engine, supported by a heavy bracket. On arriving
at the lot the engine was properly stationed with reference
to the thrash, the smoke stack was raised to a vertical position
and made fast, firewood was requisitioned from the farmer's
woodpile, and steam was generated. A heavy belt from the
engine drove the wheels of the thrash. When the engineer
blew the steam whistle the small boys who stood around to
observe operations gasped with wonder and delight.

The arrival of the thrashers always stirred the farm per-
sonnel to unwonted activity. Four men usually accompanied
the thrashing equipment, but the assistance of from four to
six other men and boys was needed to keep the wheels roll-

ing. In the kitchen the farmer's wife, with the help of her grown daughters, and perhaps of a colored woman hired for the occasion, prepared meals, which were generous in quantity if not excellent in quality. The thrashers usually had to be bedded for one night. On the second day they pulled up stakes and migrated to the next farm.

The wheat was stored in bins, and from time to time as need arose, bushels of it were carried to Ingram's mill to be ground into flour for bread. The oats were piled up on the barn floor and fed out to mules and horses.

Sorghum, popularly called millet, thrived best when planted in the moist soil of alluvial bottomlands. Its growth was lush. A half acre planted to sorghum was sufficient to supply the needs of an average family. The rows were laid off close together, and the seeds, which were small, firm, and easily handled, were strown along sparingly at the bottom of the furrow by a boy with a guano strower. Only a little cultivation was needed to enable the plant to compete successfully with grass and weeds. Sorghum grew from eight to ten feet high and produced its seed in a brush-like tassel which turned from light green to almost black when the sorghum was ripe for grinding and processing.

In addition to principal and secondary crops, every farmer who made any pretense to living well had his vegetable garden, his sweet potato patch, his melon patch, and his orchard. Even tenants had these supplements to their food supply, and no landlord ever thought of charging rent for land thus used. Irish potatoes were not in much demand. Usually two rows across the vegetable garden sufficed for the family needs. Before Irish potatoes were half grown, the housewife began to serve them, boiled with string beans and bacon, for dinner — a nourishing dish, no doubt, but not notable for savor. Only a few Irish potatoes were allowed to mature; these were kept over the winter for the next year's planting.

By the end of July all the crops had been laid by. For weeks there had been a letting up, a relaxation from strenuous labor throughout the whole community. Already school had opened at Shiloh Church for the summer session, and young children had been released from farm duties to attend. Now the older children, those between the ages of twelve and eighteen, laid aside their farm implements and trudged off to school. It was the season for picnics, all day singings, political speeches, and religious revivals; for visits to relatives living at a distance; for hunting and fishing; for love, courtship, and matrimony. If time dragged heavily on a farmer's hands, he could visit the country store or the mill, talk with other loafers, whittle sticks, chew tobacco and squirt tobacco juice, or perchance play marbles or croquet. Not until the crops were ready for the harvest was he likely to have work to do on the farm.

Meanwhile the busy housewife, with such grudging help as she could get from her menfolk, had begun the process of drying fruit for winter consumption. Apples and peaches were brought from the orchard in large pails, tediously pealed by hand and carved into thin slices which were spread out to dry in the sunshine. As batches of the sliced fruit became sufficiently dessicated, they were poured into bags of thin cotton cloth, securely tied up to prevent the encroachment of insects, and stored in a dry place, usually the kitchen. Before the fruit season was over, the menfolk of the family were loudly complaining that enough was enough; but the thrifty housewife continued to peal and slice as long as fruit was available, lest the family suffer from hunger when winter came.

By the last week of August the farmer began to observe that the silks protruding from the ears of his older corn were turning black, drying up, decaying. This was a sign that corn was maturing. If left undisturbed, the leaves of the corn stalks would shortly dry up and become of no value whatever to man or beast. To save the leaves before they were dessicated, the farmer and his older sons descended upon the corn field, stripped the leaves from the stalks, and bound them into bundles for fodder.

Fodder pullers obtained the best results when they operated in pairs. One man, walking between two rows, pulled the leaves from the stalks on his right and on his left. When he had a double handful of leaves, he deftly bound them together near their butt ends and hung the "hand," as it was technically called, on a stalk at his left. Meanwhile his partner, walking between two adjacent rows, followed suit, hanging his hand on a stalk at his right. In a short time the operation became almost automatic, and the fodder puller could talk to his partner about religion, politics, or possibly love affairs without making the mistake of hanging his hand in the wrong row.

Industrious fodder pullers got to the field early in the

morning while the grass and the weeds and the morning glory vines were still wet with dew, and the ground was sticky with moisture. They were soon wet up to their waists and their pants flopped around their legs; but as the sun mounted over them the dew disappeared, their pants dried out, and their shirts became wet with perspiration. In the tall corn of the bottomlands there was little chance for a breeze to break through and dispel the sultry heat.

After hanging six or eight hours in the sun, the fodder in the hands was "cured" and ready to be bound into bundles. At sundown, when the air became cooler and slightly moist, the pullers stopped pulling and turned their attention to "taking up" the fodder. Systematically the hands were bound into bundles, four hands to a bundle, and the bundles were tossed from the right and from the left into designated middles, where they could be easily found in the grass and cockleburs. Children home from school were now requisitioned to tote up the fodder and pile it at places where it could be conveniently reached by the wagon. A person who knew how to do the trick could carry a surprisingly large number of bundles on his head and shoulders, as he went bumping along among the corn stalks, getting trash all down his neck and in his eyes. Of course the sable curtain of night descended before the task was completed. Sticky with perspiration fodder pullers and fodder toters ate a late supper and dropped into bed without too much attention to physical cleanliness. On other days this activity was repeated until all the fodder was pulled and safely stored in the barn loft.

In late August also the farmer began to observe that the brush-like tassels of his sorghum were turning black. This was a sign that the sorghum was ready for processing. As soon as convenient he and his sons descended upon the sorghum patch and stripped the leaves from the stalks, throwing the leaves on the ground as being not worth saving for fodder. Then with sharp pocket knives the tassels were snipped off and subsequently gathered up in large baskets and hauled to the barn for cattle feed. Finally the stalks were cut down at the ground and hauled to the sorghum mill.

The sorghum mill, in its simplest form, was a heavy, cast iron machine composed of two large, upright rollers provided with cogs at the top and at the bottom and so devised as to rotate in opposite directions. The machine sat on top of a heavy, wooden framework to which it was bolted. For operational purposes, this framework could rest on the bolsters of a wagon from which the wagon bed had been removed, or it could rest on four heavy posts at the level of about three feet from the ground. The axle of one of the rollers projected some eighteen inches above the upper level of the mill and was provided with a "cuff" to which a long, wooden lever was attached. To the outer extremity of the lever a mule was hitched and driven around in a circle, causing the rollers to rotate. A man fed the stalks of sorghum between the rollers and the juice ran down a little spout into a barrel. The juice was greenish brown and had anything but an appetizing appearance.

The squeezed, or ground, stalks coming from the mill were popularly called "pummies" (pomace). Pummies, still satu-

rated with unextracted juice, quickly accumulated at the discharge side of the mill and had to be carried away by a
strong man with a pitchfork. If several crops of sorghum were
processed at the same time, the pile of discarded pummies
reached enormous proportions and was left, untouched, to
ferment and eventually to rot. No one ever thought of using
pummies for any practical purpose.

The second piece of equipment used for processing
sorghum was a large tin or copper evaporator, shaped like a
tray, about ten feet long, four feet wide, and five inches deep,
placed over a stone structure which may be best described
as an outdoor oven. The evaporator had partitions which
were somewhat like a maze. The freshly squeezed juice was
poured, in a small continuous stream, into one end of the
evaporator; the molasses was drained off at the opposite end
as the cooking was completed. The cooked molasses was a
pale brown color with high-lights of gold like the gold in
the hair of a honey blond. It had a pleasing taste and a
malty flavor reminiscent of sunshine.

It took about one hour and a half to heat the first evaporator full of juice and make it into molasses. After the first
batch, a small portion could be drawn off about every thirty
minutes.

Two persons worked continuously over the evaporator
with perforated skimmers on long handles removing the
scum from the top of the cooking molasses. The scum was
flung back into deep pits which in the course of time over-
flowed with the slimy mess. Naturally the temptation was
great for frisky young men and boys, and especially for the

loafers who were attracted to the sorghum mill, to engage in a bit of horseplay now and then and to push one another into the scum pits.

Sorghum molasses, commonly called syrup, was a standard article of diet in the Hatchet Creek community. It was poured from the syrup pitcher onto the plate, mixed with butter, and sopped with hot biscuit fresh from the oven. Every family had a syrup barrel in the smokehouse, with its convenient spigot for drawing the viscous liquid as it was needed for the table.

Cotton picking time began in early September and continued for six weeks or more. The first bolls to open were on the lower branches of the stalks and had to be picked before a heavy rainfall beat the cotton out of the bolls and scattered it on the ground to rot. Successive pickings gathered the cotton from the middle and upper branches.

When the season for picking cotton arrived the school at Shiloh Church closed, releasing the children for service in the fields. Each picker was provided with a picksack which hung at his side and also with a large basket made of white oak "splits." Stooping over until his chest almost rested on his knees, the picker walked beside the row, gathering cotton from the bolls and cramming it into his picksack. When the sack was full he emptied it into his basket. At the end of each half day the baskets were carried on shoulders to the wagon parked in the field and weighed on steelyards. If the talley showed that the picker had picked his weight in cotton during the day he was given credit for having done a good day's work.

Picking cotton was not arduous toil, but it was tedious and fatiguing to the back. Juvenile pickers amused themselves as best they could by watching the behavior of migratory birds and dancing grasshoppers. The latter would rise about four feet from the ground and, by flapping their wings, sustain themselves for a full minute without moving either forward or backward. Occasionally also a moment of pleasurable excitement was caused by a frightened cottontail springing up from its hiding place under a cotton stalk and beating a hasty retreat to more secure cover in the nearby thicket.

Cotton was hauled to the gin in capacious wagon beds, fifteen hundred pounds being considered a good load. At the gin it was unloaded by a suction process. A huge funnel-like contrivance, on the principle of the modern vacuum cleaner, was played over the top of the load and the current of air lifted the loose cotton and carried it away fast. The novelty of the operation did not fail to attract small boys who delighted to clamor aboard the wagon, loosen the cotton packed in the bed, and feed it into the omnivorous suction machine, and not infrequently a dirty cap or hat went up the funnel along with the fleecy staple.

Cotton seed was commonly regarded as hardly worth hauling home from the gin. It might be rotted down and used as fertilizer or fed to cattle, but in either case its value was questionable. Any farmer would sell a bushel of cotton seed at the gin for five cents.

Since corn was not a highly perishable product, it could be gathered at the farmer's convenience. After the fodder had been stripped from the stalks, the latter stood in the field, gaunt as flagpoles with the ears of corn flying at half-mast. At gathering time the farmer walked between two rows plucking the ears on his right and on his left and tossing them into heaps conveniently spaced along every ninth "middle." Grasping the stem of each ear with his right hand, he broke it off with his left hand in such a way as to leave the outer and rougher half of the shuck still clinging to the stalk. This method of gathering corn was called "slip-shucking." The ear retained a protective covering of soft, smooth husk which, when removed later, had some value as an inferior grade of fodder.

The cribs in which the corn was stored were usually constructed of split pine logs, with resinous sills lying flat on the ground. Termites, popularly called wood lice, had little stomach for resinous pine and wrought little damage in the community; but rats, as big as squirrels and as fat as 'possums in the persimmon season, found the corn cribs a perfect paradise. They nested in among the ears of corn; they burrowed under the sills and constructed mammoth caves into which they could scamper when danger threatened; and, although they suffered constant decimation from traps and hungry cats, the survivors continued to thrive and multiply. The remedy for the evil was to be found of course in the construction of corn cribs on yard-high posts shaped like inverted cones; but few farmers were progressive enough to be attracted by such an innovation.

Usually corn was tossed into cribs just as it came from the field, but occasionally there was a corn shucking. The farmer who wanted his corn shucked was careful to send out invitations to all the families within a two-mile radius of his residence; no family could be slighted in this matter without causing hard feelings. At the appointed hour for the festivities to begin, usually about five o'clock in the afternoon, men, women, and children came drifting in, some in buggies, some on horseback, some on foot, with eyes gleaming with pleasure at the prospect of an exciting time and a good supper. The womenfolk repaired to the house to help with the preparation of the supper or to take their places around the quilting frame; for of course there was also a quilting bee. The menfolk, as they arrived on the scene, repaired to the lot and took their places around a huge pile of corn located within easy throwing distance of the crib.

For the reception of the shucked corn the crib was thrown open by propping up the roof at a wide angle and leaving it in that position to serve as a backstop. Most of the ears struck this backstop and dropped neatly into the body of the crib, but some, thrown wild, landed in the potato patch or apple orchard beyond.

By nine o'clock the shuckers were ready to quit, whether the corn was all shucked or not. They repaired to the well in the backyard, rolled up their sleeves, and bathed their soiled hands and faces. Then in relays they took their places at the table and ate their supper. By the time all had been served the hour of midnight approached. Fretful children were piled into buggies or wagons, and all the guests departed, tired and sleepy.

The next morning the farmer, who had been the genial host of the night before, was faced with the uncongenial task of cleaning up the mess left by his guests. In his lot was a huge pile of loose shucks which had to be taken care of; shattered ears of shucked corn littered the ground; a full day's work would be required to bring order out of chaos. If, during the night, a rain had fallen, there was permanent damage to his stock of corn, a contingency which probably convinced him that a corn shucking, though a pleasant community diversion, was too costly to bear repetition.

During the winter months the enterprising farmer busied himself at various tasks — splitting rails and building or repairing fences, clearing new ground, digging ditches to drain low grounds, or perchance building a new crib out of split pine logs and roofing it with boards rived by hand with a froe. This was the season also for making contracts with tenants and making plans for the next year's crops. Restless young men, during this season between harvest and planting, dreamed of the fertile soil and the rich adventures to be had in far away Texas. An occasional bold spirit liquidated his assets, bought a railway ticket, and took off for the West, only to return in a year or two, disillusioned and bankrupt and ready to marry the girl and settle down among his friends.

LANDOWNERS AND
SHARE-CROPPERS

 MANY LANDOWNERS in the Hatchet Creek community, perhaps a majority of them, had tenants on their farms, who rented land "on shares." If the landlord furnished the land, the necessary tools and draft animals, and paid for half of the commercial fertilizer used in cotton culture, he took half of the major crops as his share of the production; if, on the other hand, the landlord furnished the land only, he took only one-third of the grain crops and one-fourth of the cotton. The first arrangement was called renting "on halves"; the other, renting "for a third and fourth." It was not the custom for a tenant to pay money or a fixed rent in kind for the use of the land.

More often than not, the tenants were the sons or the sons-in-law of the landowners of the community. When a son reached the age of twenty-one, his father "set him free" and usually gave him a horse, bridle and saddle for his economic start in life. So long as the son remained unmarried, he was likely to continue to live with the family, paying for his board and lodging by doing his share of the chores about the house and the lot. From his father he rented fifteen acres for a crop — five acres for corn and ten for cotton; at harvest time he paid a third and fourth. When he got married, he might set up housekeeping in a tenant house on his father's farm or, if that was not to his liking, he might become a tenant on another farm in the community. Now and then a young man, on getting married, preferred to leave Hatchet Creek, cross the mountain at Bull's Gap, and rent land in Talladega Valley, some twenty miles away, where the soil was by common report better suited for cotton culture. Lurking in the heart of every ambitious young man, of course, was the hope that within a few years he could save enough money from the sale of cotton to buy land and cease to be a tenant.

A few tenant families, perhaps not more than two or three in any given year, could be found in the commuinty, who had drifted in from outside and who might be classified by Yankee historians and sociologists as "poor whites." Having nothing but their labor to contribute, they rented land on halves and were seldom able, because of laziness, lack of enterprise, and perhaps sickness, to produce enough cotton and corn to make both ends meet at the end of the crop season. When a tenant of this class fell so heavily in debt to his landlord that he could never hope to pay out, he was deprived by his landlord of all his movable property except his poor clothing and his scant furniture, and set adrift to repeat the performance somewhere else.

Poor white families were usually large and the children were in many instances undernourished and afflicted with hookworm. I have a clear memory of one family which, having exhausted its supply of bacon, sorghum molasses, and corn meal, along with its credit with the landlord, was obliged to subsist for two or three weeks on sweet potatoes, until the corn in the field was hard enough for grinding at the mill. Think of it! Nothing but sweet potatoes and water for breakfast, dinner, and supper! The children of this particular family were potbellied and were sometimes seen eating the dry, red clay daubing that chinked the crevices in the rock chimney which stood outside at the end of the house. They crumbled off small chunks of the dry clay with their fingers and allowed it to melt in their mouths like fudge.

I do not remember any Negro tenant families in the community. Such Negroes as might have been seen laboring in the fields were normally hired hands.

Working for wages was not so common as renting land on shares, but the wage system was far from unknown. Farmers frequently hired, or "swapped work" with, one another for short periods. A young white man, if unmarried and destitute of working capital, might hire himself to a farmer for an entire year at a fixed monthly wage estimated in dollars; or a Negro man, either married or unmarried, might find annual employment on similar terms. The white employee normally lived in the household of his employer as a member of the family; the colored employee was regarded, and regarded himself, as several notches lower in the social scale than his employer's family: if he was unmarried he ate his meals at a separate table and slept on an inferior bed in the attic or the barn. Since the farmer had no money until his cotton was sold in late fall, the hired man customarily took at least part of his pay in other things than money. From time to time he would ask his employer for "an order on the store" for such commodities as clothing and tobacco, which would be sold to him by the merchant at credit prices, that is to say, at a profit to the merchant of thirty to forty per cent on the transaction. If the hired man was colored and married, he would ask his employer from time to time for corn, molasses, and bacon, which the employer himself furnished from his crib and smokehouse at prices high enough at least to cover the risk of future non-payment. And of course the Negro asked also from time to time for an order on the store for such commodities as flour, sugar, coffee, chewing tobacco, snuff, and clothing. At the end of the year, when the books were balanced, the white employee might have a few dollars due him, but the colored man was lucky if he made both ends meet. Indeed, unless a farmer was hard boiled with his colored help, he was likely to end the year a sadder and wiser man.

Seasonal laborers, all colored, were not an unusual spectacle in the community. A reservoir from which such labor could be drawn when needed was a Negro community commonly called The Glades, situated in the pine-clad, hilly country about halfway between Marvin's Chapel and Miller-ville. In The Glades lived several Negro landowners, with large families, eking out a bare existence on land too poor to sprout cockleburs.

One spring at the rush of the crop season my father sent word to The Glades that he could use eight or ten hoe hands as cotton choppers and that he would give each prime hand a gallon of sorghum molasses for a full day's work.

Late one morning eight Negroes, bearing empty pails, showed up in our backyard — two mothers, four adolescent daughters, and two adolescent sons — explaining that they had come to chop cotton. They had trudged the three or four miles from The Glades to our house and were in consequence already physically weary. Dropping down on whatever objects might serve as seats, they inquired about breakfast. Since Ma had not been expecting them, she could serve only the left-overs from the family breakfast, supplemented by glasses of sour buttermilk.

Shortly the labor gang was in the cotton field, each person armed with a heavy hoe. Pa explained how he wanted the work done and took the lead, bidding them all to keep pace with him. For an hour or more colored arms manipulated hoes across cotton rows with great energy, making a symphony of clacking noises on the gravelly soil. Then the pace slackened, and the labor gang disintegrated into eight dispersed stragglers.

At noon, in our backyard, the laundry bench was cleared off to serve as an improvised table, and huge platters of food were brought from the kitchen — turnip greens seasoned with hunks of bacon, pones of cornbread, biscuits, butter, molasses, and buttermilk.

That afternoon Pa chopped as much cotton as was chopped by the whole labor gang combined. Toward five o'clock there was a loud squawk from one of the mothers, and at the sound, as if the signal had long been waited for, all the

Negroes dropped to the ground, sighing and moaning. "I nevuh wuz so ti'ud in all my bawn days."

"Come on to the house," Pa called out, "and we'll have a settlement."

At the house the settlement was not easy to reach. There were tears and lamentations on the one side; irritation and angry words on the other. "Please, Mistuh, Ise wukked so ha'd."

Whether each hoe hand was paid a full gallon of molasses for services rendered that day, I do not remember; but I do know that at the end of that day Pa was a wiser man than he was the day before.

Of ready cash even prosperous farmers were destitute during most of the year. From March to November all purchases at the store were made on credit. In the spring farmers bought what they deemed necessary for making a new crop, and at all times of the year they bought clothing and such groceries as flour, sugar, coffee, and tobacco, either for their own families or for their tenants and hired hands — all on credit. In the late fall, when the cotton was sold, payment was made and the books were balanced. The marketing of the cotton crop was therefore the climax of the year's activities.

On our farm, which operated four plows, the annual yield of cotton was, on the average, around ten bales, each bale weighing around five hundred pounds. These bales, as they came from the gin, were either put on the market at once or stored in some convenient place about the premises, to be held for several weeks in the hope of a better price. Usually they were marketed at Goodwater ten miles away; but, if the rumor circulated that a better price was paid for cotton at Talladega twenty miles away, that market was given a trial.

When Pa announced his purpose to take a load of cotton to Goodwater on a certain day, weather permitting, there was a mild emotional stir in our household, particularly among the younger members, who were eager to go with him to town. At least once during the autumn I was allowed to go. I remember one such trip in early November, 1891.

During the afternoon prior to the day of departure, two or three strong men huffed and puffed two bales of cotton into position on the wagon. At daybreak the next morning the loaded wagon drawn by two mules began to roll, Pa holding the reins. For half an hour I sat beside Pa on the front end of the front bale with my feet hanging down; then, growing weary of that position, I sprawled at full length on top of the bale and whiled away the time as best I could. From time to time we passed circus posters tacked to trees and buildings along the roadside, which showed sleek women in tights swinging from trapezes or hurtling through the air, men and women standing on the backs of galloping ponies, elephants and snarling tigers. I tried to inveigle Pa into promising that he would take me to a circus sometime, but he said no, we didn't have enough money for that. As we passed farm houses or met travelers, Pa exchanged greetings with friends and acquaintances; occasionally he drew rein and tarried for a long quarter of an hour to "talk Scripture" with a brother of the Primitive Baptist faith. Not before ten o'clock did we reach our destination.

Goodwater in the early nineties was a sleepy railroad town with wooden and brick stores squatting along a dusty, littered main street. There was a small bank for the accommodation of the merchants; a hotel and livery stable for the accommodation of drummers; and two saloons where — *mirabile dictu* — those who felt the need of an uplift could buy corn liquor for a dollar a gallon.

Drab do you say? But to a small boy from a rural community Goodwater was one hundred per cent glamorous. The railroad, and the thundering locomotives with clouds of smoke belching from their funnels; the array of assorted vehicles and draft animals in the street; the merchants and clerks all wearing Sunday clothes on week days; the display of goods in the stores — bolts of cloth, new shoes, horse collars, buggy harness, saddles, canned goods, candy in the glass showcases, chewing tobacco and snuff, cheese, patent medicines, salt pork, plows and plowstocks, steel cotton ties, jute bagging, and tanks of kerosene; and, above all, the smells — odors arising from the glaze of the calicoes and the starch in the checks; from leather polish on the new shoes, the harness, and the saddles; from the cigars of "the rich city fellers"; from the tar on the cotton ties; from the jute bagging; from the decaying cabbages, sweet potatoes, and onions; from the garbage in the street; from the smoke of the locomotives — all these things combined raised Goodwater, in the eyes of the country lad, to the level of the New Jerusalem.

On our arrival in the marketplace with our load of cotton, Pa's favorite merchant came out and, with a sharp pocket knife, cut large holes in the jute bagging of the bales and extracted samples of the fleecy staple. After picking at the fibers with his fingers and making a close examination he announced: "Middling, eight point four." That is to say, he judged the cotton to be of medium grade and he was offering eight point four cents a pound for it. Pa was dissatisfied, of course, and complained that farmers could not afford to raise cotton at that price. The merchant tactfully agreed with him and shrugged off the blame for the sad plight of the Southern farmer on to the shoulders of the big cotton buyers up North. My vivid imagination at once pictured a long line-up of top-hatted, frock-coated, pig-faced gentlemen up New England way walking off with great buckets full of money squeezed from the poor cotton farmers of the South, and I experienced a deep sense of wrong and oppression.

After a while Pa took the samples of cotton fiber and canvassed the town for a higher bid, with me trotting along at his side. On such occasions as this, there was something in Pa's demeanor that made me proud of him. He stepped along briskly and confidently, and posed as a man of some distinction. People addressed him as Brother Garrett and treated him with deference. But too frequently he stopped to talk — a favorite pastime of his which bored me to extinction. After a lapse of nearly two hours we were back where we started, and the cotton was sold to the merchant who had made the first bid and was stored in his warehouse.

It was now twelve o'clock and time for lunch. Ma had fixed us a tasty lunch of biscuits and fried chicken, which we consumed with much relish.

After lunch Pa put on his spectacles and studied the shopping list which he had brought from home. The list was long, and much time was spent chaffering with the merchant over quality of goods and prices; but only one item on the list was of any interest to me, namely, a pair of new shoes. Like other children of the community, I had gone barefooted all summer. Now with the advent of frosty weather and with the opening of the winter session of school, I needed shoes. During the day I had given much thought to the matter and had screwed my courage to the point of asking Pa to buy me a pair of soft, high-topped shoes like those I had seen a few boys wearing in Goodwater. But Pa said no, brogans were good enough for any boy.

The brogan shoe was made of thick leather; the soles were fastened on with hardwood pegs that penetrated to the interior of the shoe and stood in rows along the bottom like crocodile teeth; the toes were broad; the instep was plain and innocent of any stitching to break the lines; the heavy uppers came well above the ankles of the wearer. It was, in short, an ugly, box-like, poorly constructed, and highly uncomfortable shoe. After a day or two of wear, it became hard, with deep creases across the toes and around the ankles. Only thick, home-knit socks kept the feet of the wearer from being in perpetual agony.

Pa bought me a pair of brogans.

After all the purchases had been made, Pa went with the merchant to the back of the store where the accounts were kept in huge ledgers, and made a settlement. By three o'clock in the afternoon, we had our purchases in the wagon and were rolling back toward home.

It was after nightfall when we reached home. Pa complained of a headache, which put us all on notice that he was in no mood to listen to complaints. I was dissatisfied with my brogans; Eva found the material for her new dress too cheap and tawdry; Warner was deeply hurt because Pa had failed to buy him a pair of "rubber galluses"; Wilburn found his new trousers too snug across the seat; but in the presence of that glum figure which was Pa, sitting in his accustomed corner by the fireside, reading his newspaper, we all kept silent or voiced our complaints in undertones.

Thus the day which had dawned with such high expectations was suffused with disappointment at the close. There were other market days like this in our household, and undoubtedly it had its counterpart in many another household in the community.

Occasionally Ma went to Goodwater on a shopping expedition, but she never rode thither on a load of cotton. For her accommodation the buggy was rolled out of the shed and Old Beck hitched to it; or, if several members of the family were going with her, which was usually the case, two mules were hitched to the wagon, the detachable spring seat was adjusted to the wagon bed, and kitchen chairs were taken aboard for the accommodation of those who could not find room on the spring seat.

Ma showed better judgment in the selection of clothing than Pa did, and she was much more sensitive to the complaints of her children; but her budget was limited, and, hovering in the background, there was always Pa ready to discourage unnecessary expenditures.

At least once during the market season a load of cotton went from our farm to Talladega. For this trip, which required three days, considerable preparation had to be made. An important part of the equipment was the "bow-frame and sheet," a sort of elongated hood made of canvas stretched over a framework of hickory ribs, which covered the wagon bed from stem to stern and sheltered the driver and his companion or companions from inclement weather. If the weather turned out to be fine, it was usual for the townward-bent party to stop two or three miles short of town and camp by the roadside in a sort of picnic atmosphere. If the camp site was attractive, the circle around the camp fire might be increased within a short time by the arrival of similar parties, either townward bent or homeward bound. Lunch boxes were brought from wagons and quantities of coffee prepared over the open fire. If the ground was dry and no rain threatened, bedding was spread on the carpet of pine needles and tired travelers fell asleep under the stars.

When the weather was inclement, farmers from a distance usually drove on into town at the end of the day and spent the night in the wagon yard. The wagon yard was furnished and kept up by the joint contributions of the local merchants who profited from the farmers' trade. It contained space for parking wagons and shelters of a sort for man and beast, with no fees charged or questions asked; but it was always noisy and overcrowded in bad weather, just when it was needed most. The proximity of saloons offered a sore temptation to farmers who were inclined to be bibulous to buy liquor and celebrate the harvest festival in a big way. Conditions in the wagon yard were therefore not conducive to quiet rest and sweet slumber. Sober farmers availed themselves of the accommodations only when no better place could be found.

A market day in Talladega was not unlike a market day in Goodwater. The cotton was sold and purchases were made. In the late afternoon the hooded wagon began to roll back toward home. A few miles out of town camp was made for the night by the roadside, and on the third day the return journey was completed.

In measure as the cotton was sold, settlements were made with creditors. Landowners settled with merchants, and tenants settled with landlords. If the landowner had been thrifty the books at the end of the year were likely to show a small balance in his favor. This was paid over to him in silver dollars, and taken home by him in a canvas bag. But the money in the bag was never allowed to remain out of circulation very long. It was soon invested in a mule or in additional farm land. If the tenant had likewise been thrifty the books might show a small balance in his favor. But too often the landlord had to take a tenant's corn or his cow or his pig in settlement of a deficit. The worst offenders against the principle of thrift were the poor white families who, despite the restraints and warnings of their landlords, usually contrived to consume more than they produced during the year; but fortunately such families were not numerous in the Hatchet Creek community.

SHELTER, FOOD, AND CLOTHING

 OUR DWELLING HOUSE was a frame structure of the type quite common in the rural South — two large, box-like rooms facing each other across a hallway or corridor. Each of the large rooms was flanked by two small bedrooms. There was a front porch, of course; but it did not extend the whole length of the house, being considerably abbreviated by a small bedroom at each end. Each of these rooms had but one door; none had clothes closets. There was no cellar, no bathroom, no stairway. A rock chimney at each end of the house afforded a fireplace for each of the two large rooms; there was no device for heating the four small bedrooms. As was the prevailing custom in the South, the entire house rested on pillars two or three feet above the level of the ground. Chickens, cats, and dogs wandered at will, and sometimes slept, under the floor. The walls of the house, both inside and out, were innocent of paint or varnish; nevertheless, they were of a rich brown or yellowish hue, thanks to the influence of age and weather.

One of the large rooms was used as the family living room.

In it were the following articles of furniture: two beds, in one of which Pa and Ma slept; several stout hickory chairs, straight, heavy, and painted black; a heavy round table, home-made and painted black, on Pa's side of the fireplace, on which stood the kerosene lamp and on which lay a small New Testament, Bunyan's *Pilgrim's Progress*, and perhaps another dust covered book or two; a heavy homemade wooden chest against the wall on Ma's side of the fireplace, painted black, in which Pa kept his land deeds and other valuable articles, and which he kept securely locked; a tall clothes press (or wardrobe), homemade and painted black, in a far corner, behind one of the beds, in which Ma kept the family's clean linen and from which she distributed the same on Sunday mornings after the various members of the household had had their sponge baths. On nails driven into the pine board walls hung a variety of articles: hats, coats, a small calendar, Grier's Almanac, and what you will; on the mantelpiece, which was painted black, stood the clock and on each side of the clock could be found whatever you were looking for, be it a nail, a file, a box of pills, a bottle of patent medicine, or Pa's specs. The employment of black as the motif of interior deco-ration was not unusual in the community. It reflected, at least in theory, the religious mood of the family. A somber room with dark furniture acted as a damper on gay and frivolous spirits.

The other large room was the parlor. In it were two of the family's best beds, the bureau with its mirror and comb, several store-bought chairs, including a rocker, and a center table. On the center table lay the big family Bible with the fringed ends of its wide silken "marker" hanging far down on two sides. Draped over the pillows on the beds were pillow shams, embroidered in red and blue on a white background and inscribed with such beautiful sentiments as "Good Night" and "Sweet Rest." On the mantel were various sorts of bric-a-brac thought to be decorative.

Every farmhouse of any importance in the community had its parlor. This was the guest room where visitors were bedded down for the night. Here young people gathered at appropriate times to talk and laugh and possibly to sing. In the parlor the adult daughter of the family entertained her boy friend on Sunday afternoons or evenings. The young man trotted up on horseback, or more likely on mule back, hitched his steed to a shade tree outside the front gate, and was received at the parlor door in the hallway by the young lady who took particular pains to appear nonchalant.

In our house the floors, walls, and ceilings of all the rooms were made of wide, fine-grained pine boards. There were no carpets on the floors, not even a small rug beside any of the beds; nor was there any paper on the walls or ceilings. Once or twice a year, preferably in the fall and the spring, there was a general house cleaning. The feather beds and straw beds and quilts were given a thorough sunning; the furniture was taken out into the yard, scalded with boiling water and afterwards, when it was dry again, swabbed ·in the cracks and crevices with stiff feathers steeped in spirits of turpentine to exterminate any bed bugs (we called them "chinches") that might be hiding there; even the cracks and crevices in the walls were turpentined for the same purpose.

Then followed the scouring of the floors with warm water, soap and fine white sand. The mop was homemade and heavy and stuffed with corn shucks. After the cleansing process had been completed, the doors and windows were left open for several hours for the house to dry out.

Several steps from the back door of our dwelling house was the combination kitchen-dining room. This was a large, rectangular building constructed of split pine logs mortised together at the corners, with the flat sides of the logs turned inward. After the logs were in place, a broad ax had been used to hew the flat sides smooth and plumb. To cover the inevitable cracks between logs, thin pine boards were nailed on the inside. At one end of the large room was a rock fireplace, near which stood the wood burning cook stove with its pipe running straight up through the roof. There was no ceiling. In the center of the room stood the dining table; against the wall near the stove were the flour barrel, the meal barrel, a small table, and a wooden tray for kneading dough. At the end opposite the fireplace, and encroaching upon Pa's place at the table, stood the ponderous loom. To insulate the room for winter use, as well as to embellish its interior, Ma pasted old newspapers on the walls. One could sit at the table or at any other point of vantage and read "Atlanta Weekly Constitution" in a score of different places.

We always called this the kitchen, never the dining room. So firmly has the idea become fixed in my mind that kitchen and dining room are synonymous terms that, after the lapse of sixty years, I still occasionally get them confused and call the dining room the kitchen.

Our yard spread out over a considerable area. Along the front of it, paralleling the road, ran a paling fence, which, if you are a Yankee, you would call a picket fence. This fence was cut in twain by a conspicuous and somewhat decorative front gate. Less ornate fences completed the enclosure. Oak shade trees stood here and there, but no attempt was ever made to keep a lawn.

In the backyard was the well, covered by a roof of rived boards which rested upon four tall, sturdy posts. The well had its curb, its windlass, and its oaken bucket. Only moss was needed to give the bucket the poetic glamor of Samuel Woodworth's sentimental song.

It was usual for a family to have a water shelf on the back porch, but since our house had no back porch, our water shelf was of necessity placed on the front porch. On the shelf were a cedar bucket, a wash pan (we never said "wash basin"), and a dipper. The dipper might be a store bought article made of tin or enameled iron, but more likely it was made from a long handled gourd or from the half shell of a coconut mounted on a wooden handle. Children were carefully taught not to put the dipper back in the bucket after they had finished drinking, but to put it down beside the bucket or hang it on a nail driven into the nearby wall.

Before each meal all male members of the family were required, and male guests were expected, to go to the wash shelf and wash their hands and faces. On a nail driven into the nearby wall, a towel hung by a loop sewed to one corner. All used the same towel without detaching it from the nail. Then the adults went to the mirror in the parlor and combed their hair with the family comb. Washing facilities of a sort could also be found in the kitchen, but the menfolk were not encouraged to go there for their ablution because their presence interfered with the serving of the meal.

In the absence of modern bathroom facilities, the delicate question arises as to where we betook ourselves in response to the calls of nature. As I remember, that problem never offered any difficulties at all. There were numerous places where one could find seclusion — at the lot, behind the smokehouse, in the underbrush along the zigzag rail fences, in the nearby thickets, or out in the cultivated fields. In the whole community I do not remember ever seeing a conventional backhouse.

In the summertime, through the open door and windows, flies swarmed into the kitchen. When the table was set for a meal, the plates were turned bottom upwards in the interest of cleanliness and sanitation. When the meal began, each member of the family turned his plate over and fanned the flies away as best he could with his hands. On special occasions, when guests were present, one of the waiting children stood near the table and waved a long leafy branch from a peachtree over the festive board. In some homes a fan-like contrivance, as wide as the table and tipped with long strips of paper, was used. It was suspended from the ceiling or overhead joist and operated by a cord in the hand of the housewife from her place at the table. But such a contrivance was not effective over the full length of a long table. Pa complained, when it was tried at our table, that Ma was just shooing the flies down on him.

In our dwelling house flies were not so numerous as in the kitchen, but they buzzed about in sufficient numbers to make a siesta well-nigh impossible.

In case of sickness, it was the custom in the community for someone to sit by the bedside of the patient and "mind the flies away." Mothers with young babies sometimes covered cradles with a netting called "mosquito bar" when the babies were sleeping, but nobody ever so much as thought of the possibility of screening the doors and windows. Dr. Darby, when he came to the community, sometimes mildly hinted that flies were unsanitary, but even he could think of no effective way to get rid of them. At his house there were just as many flies as there were in any other farmhouse.

When cold weather came the flies of course disappeared, but other discomforts arose to plague us. Not the least of these was the chill of our living quarters.

On winter evenings after supper our family formed a semicircle in front of the open fire in the living room. Pa and Ma sat with their backs to the wall on either side of the fireplace and kept reasonably warm; but the rest of the family sat with their backs to the open door leading into the hallway, turning first one side and then the other to the fire to keep warm, for of course there was a steady draft from the open door to the fireplace.

Why not close the door into the hallway and thereby eliminate the draft? Habit or custom, probably. Members of the family passing constantly to and fro through the door thoughtlessly and carelessly left it open, until the habit was formed, the tradition established. In my youth we used a chair or some other article of furniture to keep the door propped open. Some families in the community used a brick or a smooth rock or possbily a conch shell for the purpose. When visitors called, they naturally entered without knocking, since there was no closed door to knock at; they merely announced their arrival by calling out cheerfully from the open doorway "How're y'all?"

Toward eight o'clock on winter evenings drooping eyelids signalized the advent of bedtime. We boys removed our shoes and socks in the living room while we sat by the fire and tossed them aside. Then we trudged off to bed, bare feet on cold floors, across the hallway, into the dark and chilly bedroom, where we removed our coats and pants, dropping them on the floor, and crawled, shivering, under the covers, with our ordinary underwear serving as pajamas. Pa was usually the last to retire. Before doing so, he closed the living room door and fastened it on the inside by dropping the latch into the staple driven into the doorfacing.

Next morning at five o'clock Pa reached out from under the bed covers, raised the latch, partially opened the door, and called out:

"Mitch! Mitch-ull! Mitch-u-u-ull!"

"Sir?" I answered from my warm feather bed.

"Come! Get up and start the fires."

Crawling out of bed on to the cold floor I slipped into my pants (the coat could wait till later) and started the fire in the living room. Fortunately dry resinous pine makes excellent kindling. On to the roaring flame I tossed oak and hickory logs and soon had the room warm. Then I proceeded across the backyard to the kitchen and started a fire in the cook stove. By that time the rest of the family were getting up, and it was another day.

For breakfast Ma kneaded dough in a wooden tray and baked a large panful of biscuits; she ground freshly roasted coffee beans in the coffee mill attached to the wall and made a pot of coffee; she fried several thin slices of ham or bacon and made gravy, sometimes milk gravy; during the summer season, if guests had spent the night with us, or if it were Sunday morning, she more than likely served a big platter of fried chicken instead of ham or bacon. To these dishes she would add a bowl of butter fresh from the churn, the syrup pitcher full of sorghum molasses, and perhaps a large pitcher of buttermilk. Since sweet milk was needed in butter-making, it was seldom served as a table beverage except to small children.

When breakfast was ready Ma rang a small hand bell to summon the family. When all were seated, Pa at one end of the table and Ma at the other, there was a signal for all to bow their heads and keep quiet while Pa said the blessing. After the lapse of sixty years the words of that blessing, which seldom varied, are graven on my memory: "Our Father, forgive our sins and give us thankful hearts for these and all Thy blessings. We ask for Christ's sake. Amen." Close inspection will reveal that in the first sentence the meaning would be more accurately expressed by the insertion of the word "other" before "blessings"; but on the whole the invocation defies improvement. It is comprehensive and pat and has the priceless quality of brevity. Occasionally through the years I have been startled by a kind hostess asking me to offer thanks for the blessing of a meal; and, before my mind could begin to function, my embarrassed lips would begin to murmur automatically the well-remembered words of my father's invocation.

Adult members of the family generally used knives and forks, though not too expertly, to convey food to their mouths; children used their fingers, sopping fragments of biscuit in a mixture of butter and molasses. Coffee was poured from the cup into the saucer to cool prior to imbibition. Only adults with cast iron stomachs could eat and successfully digest the fried slices of home processed bacon.

The menu of the midday meal varied somewhat with the seasons: in the summer, corn pone, buttermilk, boiled vegetables seasoned with bacon, and deep dish fruit pies; in the autumn, as garden vegetables diminished, sweet potatoes bulked large as a staple food; in the spring there were still pork products, to which one could add dried-fruit pies. Supper at eventide usually consisted of leftovers from the midday meal.

Of course at ordinary mealtimes the entire family gathered at the table and pursued the usual routine; but on special occasions, when an extra quality of food was served and guests were present, the small childern had to wait until the adults had dined. I still have poignant memories of sitting or leaning on the loom in our kitchen and watching with hungry eyes the choicest pieces of fried chicken disappear down adult gullets. Once when I cried out in my anguish that our guest, Brother Gosden, was eating up all the butter,

Pa turned in his chair and without a word slapped me back under the loom.

Despite, however, the implication of the outcry in the episode just mentioned, we always had plenty to eat at our house and extended a generous hospitality to all who came. Any member of the family was at liberty, without giving advance notice, to bring in a friend or two for a meal. To adult guests Pa's stock remark, after saying the blessing, was: "Just turn over your plates and help yourselves, if you can find anything on the table fit to eat." Everyone present of course, both family and guests, understood the remark to be made in a spirit of modesty; but today I wonder what my wife would say to me behind the domestic "iron curtain," if I were to make a crack like that to a guest.

Our milk supply came from two or three scrawny cows, the care and milking of which devolved almost exclusively upon the womenfolk of the family. Ma usually did the milking until Eva, three years my senior, was large enough to be assigned that chore. For some reason — I always attributed it to personal spite — Eva insisted that I go along with her to feed the cows and hold off the calves during the milking process. How I hated that sort of thing! The smell of the cows, the slop under foot, and the general nastiness! But there was no escape, for Eva's request was backed up by parental fiat.

On arriving at the cowshed I took a large pailful of cotton seed from the cotton seed bin, poured about a gallon of the seed into the feed trough of one of the stalls, mixed in about a quart of corn meal, and then admitted the cow to the stall.

While the cow ate greedily, the calf was admitted and for about half a minute was allowed to do what a calf is supposed to do. The nuzzling and sucking of the calf, induced the cow to "give down her milk." At the end of about half a minute I placed a rope halter over the calf's nose and head and, with many a grunt and tug and blasphemous thought unspoken, I dragged it outside the stall and kept it there while Eva milked the cow. When that task was completed, the calf was released and allowed to return to its mother; and the process was repeated in an adjoining stall until all the cows were milked.

At our house the second milking of the day was always done, winter and summer, before supper. On Sunday afternoons, when Eva's boy friend fell into the habit of lingering late in the parlor, I would go to the kitchen for the pail and feed pan and, with loud clang of pail on pan, I would stride through the hallway to the parlor door and sing out: "Milking time!" The nuisance value of the stunt was enormous. What kept Eva from murdering me, after the embarrassed leave-taking of her boy friend, was Ma's solid support of my contention that milking should always be done at milking time.

One of our cows — we called her Ole Heff — was such a scrawny beast that she had to walk twice in the same place to cast a shadow. Every year she gave birth to progeny and every day of the year she gave fully a quart of bluish milk. As I look back over the years, I have not the slightest doubt that Ole Heff was a prolific nursery of tuberculosis germs. If there had been scientific inspection of milk cows in the Hatchet Creek community in those days, I am convinced that my brother Warner would have been saved much suffering and the loss of his leg.

Christmas was the time for a real spending orgy, when items of luxury, like oranges, raisins, and nuts, were purchased. On Christmas eve night children hung their stockings to the mantelpiece in the living room, and on Christmas morning they waked up to find their stockings full of goodies. Mothers usually stripped off the orange peelings and passed the fruit around in segments, and carefully laid the peelings aside to be used throughout the year as flavoring for cakes, custards, and puddings. Sugary raisins made a special appeal to children, who pulled the brown bunches out of their stockings on Christmas morning with more excitement than they showed for the striped peppermint stick candy. And opening the coconut was a real adventure. First there was the sport of punching in the soft eyes in order to draw off the richly flavored milk. Then followed the sawing of the nut in two at the equator. One half of the shell, if the edges had not been chipped by the sawing, could be used to make an excellent bowl for a dipper.

The clothes which my family wore during week days were made, for the most part, of store-bought cloth and kept in repair by my mother. But the ponderous loom in the kitchen was far from a museum piece. Ma resorted to it frequently enough to keep the family supplied with jeans, a coarse woolen cloth of heavy weave, which was ordinarily used for making winter trousers. Once or twice, as I remember, my sister Lee Anna borrowed the loom and kept it at her house for months at a time, for the purpose of weaving an all-cotton cloth from which she made coarse sheets and pillow cases for her beds. Such cloth had the advantage of being durable and, when dyed purple or green, colorful enough to conceal the need of frequent laundering.

Cloth making devolved entirely upon the womenfolk of the family. Cotton was carded by hand and made into rolls a little larger than a man's thumb and about ten inches long, but wool was commonly carded by machinery. After the annual harvest of wool from the family's flock had been thoroughly cleansed, it was sent miles away to some indefinite place called "the factory" and brought back in the form of rolls a yard long. The spinning was done by an old fashioned spinning wheel. As the spinner twirled the wheel, making it hum loud enough to be heard several hundred yards away, the rolls were twisted into thread which was then "run up" on the "broach." When the carding and spinning were done, the thread had to be dyed, sized, warped, beamed, harnessed, sleyed, and woven. Each of these words had a specific technical meaning which was well understood by housewives.

Not all the thread that came from the spindle of the humming wheel, however, was used for cloth making. Indeed the greater part of it was used for knitting socks and stockings. Ma was always knitting when she had nothing else to do. When she called on a neighbor she took her knitting along with her. On winter evenings, when she sat in her corner by the fireside, she kept her fingers busy with her knitting needles. She could never relax, she often said, without something for her idle fingers to do. What was true of Ma was true of other housewives. All had to knit constantly to keep their families supplied with hosiery. There may have been store-bought socks and stockings in the community, but I do not remember ever seeing any.

What did men and boys wear as everyday work clothes? In the summertime the principal garments were a cotton shirt and a pair of cotton trousers held up by wide suspenders. Boys prior to the age of adolescence went barefooted, but adolescent and adult males usually wore socks and brogan shoes. At bedtime dirty feet were washed in the family washpan taken from the water shelf, trousers were removed, and both men and boys slipped into bed with nothing on but the shirts which they had worn all day. The usual headgear was a cheap, broad brimmed palmetto hat which effectively shaded the face but which had a tendency to flop down and interfere with vision. Young men of courting age took great pains to protect their skin from suntan. To that end they wore, while working in the fields, the broad brimmed hat already mentioned, a large cotton handkerchief around the neck, and some sort of improvised gloves on the hands. A skin free from suntan and palms free from calluses were considered the hallmarks of gentility.

In winter the trousers were woolen, more than likely; the hat felt. Small boys now wore shoes and socks. Adolescent and adult males put on long, cotton-cloth drawers. This garment was held together at the waist by a large white button; at each ankle was a slit six or eight inches long. To the corners of each slit were sewed two strong cotton strings. When the wearer slipped into the drawers he buttoned the garment at the waist and stooping over he overlapped the edges of the slits snugly around his ankles and bound them with the strings. The coat commonly worn in winter was an old store-bought coat, which had become too shabby for Sunday wear. Store-bought denim overalls, so common today, were unknown to the community.

Feminine attire on week days tended to be sombre and loose-fitting. The distinctive feature was the long skirt worn by adolescent and adult women, which afforded ample coverage for the ankles. The "unmentionables" — correct me if I go wrong — were the chemise (pronounced "shimmy"), which covered the shoulders and dropped below the hips, and a pair of loose-fitting drawers which dropped to the knees. Over the latter garment but under the dress was the petticoat which hung at the waist and reached to the ankles. In winter, adult women sometimes wore a striped woolen petticoat called a balmoral. The feminine counterpart of the man's coat was the cloak which was worn only in winter. The dress of small girls did not differ essentially from that of adult women except that the skirt was shorter and in summer the shoes and stockings were missing.

Woman's crowning glory, as we have often heard, is her hair. In my youth all members of the fair sex, both young and old, wore their hair long and kept it combed and dressed without benefit of beauty parlors. Little girls wore their hair in two braids down the back; adolescent and adult women coiled their hair into neat buns on the back or the top of the head. For variety, little girls and young ladies sometimes wore bangs.

During week days the prevailing feminine headgear was

the sunbonnet. The rigid brim of the sunbonnet projected three or four inches out front and, curving downward, covered completely both sides of the face; at the back was a small ruffled cape which loosely covered the neck; two strips of soft cloth tied in a bow knot under the chin kept the bonnet snugly in place on the head. Young ladies sometimes managed to look chic in neat sunbonnets, but women over forty-five seemed to take pride in wearing bonnets that signalized none too subtly the end of youthfulness. The badge of a really old woman was a black, stave-ribbed bonnet that looked like a pall. The restricted vision and muffled ears incidental to bonnet-wearing never seemed to be a serious handicap. Maids and matrons and elderly dames always managed to see all that was worth seeing and to hear more than was good for them or the community.

Cotton garments, particularly underwear and hosiery, had of course to be washed frequently.

Our wash bench with its wooden tubs, and the "battling block" with its "battling stick," stood in the backyard not far from the well. Nearby stood the big cast iron washpot.

On Monday morning of each week, weather permitting, Ma and Eva took the huge bundle of family washing to the backyard and sorted the garments roughly into two or three different piles. Then the washing began. First the clothes were well smeared with soft soap and boiled in the washpot. Then, while still hot and steaming, they were carried on the end of the battling stick to the battling block where they were thoroughly pounded with the battling stick. After the pounding, they were smeared with soap again and dropped

into a tub half full of warm water. Here they were thoroughly scrubbed by hand and passed on to the rinsing tub half full
of cold water. Then the water was wrung out of them and
they were hung in the sun to dry. It was my job, when
a small boy, to fill up the washpot on Monday mornings, build
a fire under and around it to heat the water, do the battling,
and make myself generally useful in carrying pails of water
from the well to the tubs.

For washing clothes, dishes, kitchen utensils, and other
things, the mother of the family was expected to make the
necessary soap. The essential ingredients of soft soap were
alkali and grease.

Behind our kitchen was the ash hopper, shielded from the
rain by a movable cover. Into the hopper, during the winter
months, were dumped the ashes from the fireplaces. At some
convenient time during the late spring or early summer, Ma
poured quantities of water into the hopper to leach out the
lye, which she caught in pails as it trickled from the bottom
of the hopper. The lye, mixed with waste fat which had been
carefully hoarded throughout the year for "soap grease," was
then boiled in the washpot and reduced to a ropy consistency,
greenish in color and slightly malodorous. When stirred in
water this soft soap made a generous supply of suds and was
an excellent detergent. Ma always kept her soft soap in a
large earthen jar, from which she ladled it out into small
containers for immediate use.

It goes without saying that all the men of the community
were valiant and all the women virtuous.

Fashion and personal pride demanded that men wear

some sort of beard. Young sprigs of the male sex who aspired to cut a wide swath with the young ladies tended their mustaches with the greatest care, waxing them on Sundays and twisting the ends into neat spirals at the corners of the mouth. Middle-aged men usually wore full beards, though some of the beards could hardly be called up to standard; men who were really old were disposed to cling to the hirsute adornment of an earlier generation — smooth lips and jowls with whiskers under the chin à la Jefferson Davis or Horace Greeley. Our community doctor, as befitted a professional man, wore sideburns.

For Sunday wear the young man, as soon as he could sprout a respectable mustache, provided himself with a store-bought frock coat and a sporty hat, perhaps a derby. On his way to and from church, whether walking or riding horseback, he carried an umbrella in the summertime to protect his skin from the sun's bright rays. The young lady, when dressed up for Sunday, wore her hair neatly coiled on her head and her bangs fashionably frizzled. Over this coiffure she wore a sailor hat from which draped a diaphanous veil. To enhance the whiteness and softness of her face, she applied powder in liberal quantities; if store-bought powder was not available, flour from the flour barrel in the kitchen could be used as a satisfactory substitute. Her leg-o'-mutton sleeves stuck up at the outer points of her shoulders to the level of her ears, and her long skirt swept the ground. A close fitting corset gave her the wasp-like waist, and "falsies" at the breast and a modest bustle at the hips provided the curves, which fashion demanded. In the summertime, on her way to and from church, she carried a silken parasol fringed with frothy lace.

SICKNESS AND DEATH

 THE HATCHET CREEK community was of course afflicted with many of the ills that flesh is heir to.

It was quite common for the barefooted children to have "the toe eetch" or "the ground eetch" and to pass with their loose bowel movements hundreds of tiny white worms, alive and kicking; but parents were not greatly disturbed by these symptoms.

It was quite common also for barefooted children to have stone bruises on their heels and infected sores on their feet, legs, and hands, and to complain of "kernels" in their groins and armpits; but for the treatment of such trivial ailments as these the advice of a physician was not deemed necessary. The mother of a small boy who had snagged his bare foot on a rusty nail simply cleansed the wound, bandaged it with a strip of cotton cloth saturated with spirits of turpentine, and waited for nature to effect a cure. I never heard of anyone in the community having tetanus or serious blood poisoning.

When a child waked up at night crying with earache, the mother slipped out of bed, went to the kitchen and made a poultice of hot meal dough, and had the child pillow the aching ear on the poultice. The remedy was usually effective. When a child waked up in the morning with a sore throat and racking cough, the mother brought in a heaping spoonful of sugar dampened down with spirits of turpentine and insisted that the sufferer swallow the evil-smelling, evil-tasting mixture. It burned, as I can testify, like the woods on fire. How effective the remedy was is open to question. The cold always ran its course, afflicting the victim with red eyes and a dripping nose. The discharge from the nose sometimes hung down like the loose end of a rope.

"Wipe your nose," was a frequent and urgent request from parents and teachers. But how was a small boy to keep his nose clean when he never carried a handkerchief? The sleeve was the answer. The jeans sleeve of a winter coat might rasp like a file when drawn across the upper lip and nose, but it was in a measure effective. What the sleeve looked like after a long siege of cold is another question.

Headaches, toothaches, and chronic backaches were the monopoly of the adults. The remedy for headache was a hot liniment applied to the forehead and temples, or sliced red peppers soaked in vinegar and held in place on the forehead and temples by a bandage. Toothache was a far more serious matter. No care was ever taken of the teeth and, in the absence of a dentist, they decayed, broke off, developed ulcers, and sometimes made life thoroughly miserable. Dr. Darby, when he came to the community to practice medicine, knew nothing of dentistry; but, pressed by the supreme need of giving relief to sufferers from toothache, he bought a pair of forceps and began to extract teeth in accordance with the rule "Go at it and do it." Once I stood by and watched him pull two teeth for Aunt Mariah. At each extraction she made a horrible sound, between a scream and a gurgle, which was not pleasant to hear. Nearly all middle-aged people of the community had gaps in their teeth, and old people commonly had no teeth at all.

Occasionally one heard elderly people, particularly in the springtime, complain of having bad blood. Obviously the quickest way to get rid of bad blood was to open a vein and drain out a pint or two of the polluted stuff.

Dr. Darby pooh-poohed the idea of blood-letting, but his advice was not always followed.

One of my earliest recollections is that of Pa sitting in a chair on our front porch with the shirt sleeve of his left arm rolled above the elbow. A man, whose name I do not remember, whetted the thin blade of a lancet and pushed the blade through a cork bottle stopper until perhaps half an inch protruded. This was to gauge the depth of the incision. Then the man found a vein in Pa's arm above the elbow, popped the point of the lancet into it, and stood back to watch the blood flow. At first the blood spurted out in a tiny stream, then trickled down the arm and poured off the finger tips. After a while the flow stopped of its own accord, and the washpan, which had been set to catch the blood, showed that a pint or more had been drained off. What happened afterwards I do not remember, but I suppose Pa got well of what ailed him.

A remedy for chronic backache, widely advertised in the

newspapers, was the "porous plaster," a rather large piece of linen cloth smeared on one side with a viscid substance of some sort, which was designed to adhere to the back, covering the region of the pain. Porous plasters were popular with nervous, overwrought mothers who wore them for weeks and even months without renewal.

In a community where mongrel dogs flourished and were especially cherished by boys and young men, mad dog scares were fairly common. No person in the community, so far as I know, was ever bitten by a mad dog, but there was always the possibility.

The surest remedy for mad dog bite was the "mad stone," a substance of indeterminate composition, about the size of a walnut and porous like honey comb, taken from the maw of a wild deer which had been shot down on the mountainside long ago by someone's grandfather. None of my acquaintances had ever seen a mad stone, but they had heard that Sam Russell over in Talladega Valley had one and that Willie McGehee over beyond Millerville had another. To all of us it was comforting to know that this specific remedy for the dread infection was available.

If a person was bitten by a dog suspected of being mad, he or she was to be taken immediately to the precious stone, which, if the dog was indeed rabid, would stick fast when applied to the wound. When its pores became full of poison, the stone dropped off. When washed in warm milk and water, thus leaching out the poison, it would stick to the wound again. If at the first application the stone failed to stick on the wound, so the belief ran, the dog was not mad;

if after several successful applications and repeated cleansings the stone stopped sticking, the poison was all extracted and the patient had nothing more to fear.

Constipation was of course the monopoly of no age group. It was especially prevalent in the wintertime when the daily diet consisted of cornbread, hot biscuits, sorghum molasses, bacon and white gravy, which clogged the physical system with poisons. The symptoms were lack of appetite, bad breath, coated tongue, and fever. The remedy, whether the sufferer was an adult or a young child, was a dose of castor oil or Epsom salts or calomel or possibly one of several varieties of pills. If colitis resulted from the administration of any of these drastic purgatives, the cause of the trouble was never recognized or understood.

Spring was the season, not only for cleaning house and for cleaning the bushes and briers from fence corners and ditch banks, but also for cleaning the intestinal tract.

At some time during the early spring Pa called for the little tin box that contained the family's supply of calomel. On the tip of the blade of his pocket knife he measured out the dosage for each member of the family, including himself. Each dose was mixed in a teaspoonful of molasses and swallowed. There was no taste except that of the molasses.

Then followed a period of ten days or more when we were forbidden to eat certain things lest we become "salivated." Naturally the things that a small boy was forbidden to eat were exactly those things that he craved most after a long winter diet of starchy foods and molasses, such as half grown June apples in the orchard and wild onions and "sour grass" in the fields. I never saw anyone who had been salivated, but I understood from what Ma said that the inside of the mouth of a salivated person became one festering sore and that all the teeth dropped out. No devout Catholic or Episcopalian ever observed Lent any more scrupulously than we children observed that period of abstinence which followed our spring doses of calomel.

Members of my family were not given to the consumption of patent medicines in great quantities, but Ma always kept a few bottles on hand. The following were the most popular brands, though of course we did not keep all of these on hand at the same time: McElree's Wine of Cardui, Thedford's Black Draught, Hood's Sarsaparilla, Dr. Pierce's Favorite Prescription, S. S. S., Lydia E. Pinkham's Vegetable Compound, and various sorts of pills, liniments, and tonics. When Ma, for example, felt "a bit under the weather" or "down in the mouth," she reached for the bottle on the mantlepiece in the living room and took a swig of Sarsaparilla or Wine of Cardui. It tasted strongly of herbs and caused her to make a wry face; but presently it gave a warm, cheerful glow to her whole system. No wonder she recommended it highly for the relief of aches and pains. How could she know that the swig she had taken from the bottle was equivalent in alcoholic content to a good-sized toddy?

Dr. Darby always frowned on mothers who gave paregoric to babies. But the temptation was great; the drug was cheap and its sale was unrestricted. At the approach of noon, when dinner had to be ready for the hungry husband, a mother with an exhausted body and frayed nerves might easily be forgiven if she reached for the paregoric bottle and gave two drops to the fretful child at her knees and a similar dose to the baby in the cradle crying with colic. It was such a comfort to know, after a morning of storm and stress, that both of the children were peacefully sleeping.

Pain in the abdomen was a common ailment which attracted little attention unless the pain continued for several hours. In this case a purgative was indicated, on the assumption that there was something in the alimentary tract that needed to be expelled. If the purgative failed to give relief in due time, it was in order to send for Dr. Darby.

If, on arriving at the bedside, Dr. Darby found the patient still in pain, he would open his medicine case, take out a vial, shake from it a morphine tablet, and call for a glass of water.

"Just place this on your tongue," he would say to the patient, "and rinch it down with a swallow of water."

While the drug was taking effect, he would count the pulse and take the temperature of the patient, inquire about bowel movements and about the nature of the purgative that had been administered. Then with the air of a man who had the situation well in hand, he would relax in an easy chair and for half an hour or more exude optimism and geniality. Rising from the chair to end the call he would again consult his medicine case, putter around with several vials, pour out a small quantity of white or brown powder, divide it carefully into doses, and fold each neatly in a thin slip of paper about half the size of a cigarette paper.

"Give John [or whatever the patient's name was] one of these powders every four hours. And, O yes; if his pain returns, give him another one of these morphine tablets. I will look in again sometime tomorrow to see how he is getting on."

In many cases John could be counted on to recover from his intestinal disturbance and be up and about the next day when the doctor returned. But there were dreadful stories, not easily forgotten, of patients who suddenly grew worse and quickly died, in spite of morphine tablets and doses of white or brown powders. These fatal cases Dr. Darby diagnosed, usually after the event, as "cramp colic." How could you blame him? In that day nobody had ever heard of appendicitis.

In the treatment of typhoid fever Dr. Darby was regarded by the people of the community as especially adept. When summoned to attend a fever patient, he assumed an attitude of watchful waiting and gave very little medicine; but he prescribed an abstemious diet and sternly forbade the patient to drink more than a few spoonfuls of water each day. The common report was that nearly all his patients survived.

But Dr. Darby's greatest service to the community was rendered in connection with the birth of babies.

It was not the custom in the community for an expectant mother to receive professional care and advice prior to the onset of the birth pangs; but the moment the baby signalized his intention to emerge into the world of sunshine and bird-song, there was a wave of excitement in the household and soon a man on mule back was galloping for the doctor, no matter what the time of day or night, no matter what the weather. And Dr. Darby on his powerful saddle horse could be counted on to come galloping to the rescue in response to the summons.

I well remember the excitement that occurred early one morning down at the ford of Hatchet Creek near our house. Rain had been falling for several days and the creek was overflowing its banks. Men on the other side were shouting something hard to understand because of the distance and the noise of the stream, and men on my side were shouting back. After a while I saw a horseman ride into the smooth, shallow water on the other side and head in our direction. Slowly the water came up to the horse's flank and then to the saddle. Near midstream, where the current was swift, the horse stumbled, lost footing, began to plunge and struggle; but the rider clung to the saddle. Presently the horse found firm footing once more, reached shallow water, and came dashing up to our group, snorting and trembling with excitement. The rider was Dr. Darby answering a call to a maternity case.

On reaching our group, the doctor dismounted. While someone held the reins of his horse, he huffed and puffed, took off his professional frock coat and wrung the water from its tails, took off his shoes and wrung out his socks, and noted that his medicine case, though dripping with water, was still in place across the back of the saddle. Presently he mounted again and went galloping off, just a country doctor answering a call for professional service. His fee for a maternity case was five dollars payable in the autumn when the cotton was sold. In many a case the prospect was slim indeed that the fee would ever be paid.

In the Resurrection Morning, when the saints of earth

take wing and fly to heaven, St. Peter, I am sure, will ask the angels to make room on the front seats for the old fashioned country doctors, who, to be sure, had little knowledge of anatomy and medicine when measured by present day standards, but who had a sense of duty and were unselfish in their humble efforts to alleviate human suffering.

When sickness occurred in a family, neighbors were always sympathetic and eager to be of service. If word got around that the patient was low, they made it a point to drop in on the afflicted family at frequent intervals and sit around for hours at a time, talking in hushed tones and looking sad and depressed. When Uncle Nat Grice was in his last illness, as I well remember, the room in which he lay was made especially gloomy by hanging quilts over the windows, and there was in the room also an odor of stale air and fecal matter.

When a person died, the relatives of the deceased were expected to weep and wail a right smart to indicate their grief, lapsing at intervals into a sort of comatose condition. Good neighbors "laid out" the body, that is, washed and dressed it for burial, and laid it out on the best bed in the parlor with the eyes closed and the hands folded across the chest. Since one night at least always intervened between death and burial, it was the custom to sit up with the corpse from twilight till dawn. This last service was often performed by a group of young people of courting age who dropped in at nightfall, packed the aggrieved family off to bed, and took over the premises for a quiet social gathering. If the season was summer, they could sit on the front porch, talk, and play games; if winter, they could sit in the living room or kitchen by the open fire. There was nothing especially solemn about "sitting up with the body."

As soon as possible after the death angel had struck, good neighbors turned their attention to making the coffin and digging the grave.

Pa was quite adept at making coffins. I have hung around our blacksmith shop, which was provided with vise, drawing knife and other tools for working in wood, and watched him make several, including Uncle Nat's and, I think, Grandpap's. First he took careful measurements of the body from head to foot and across the chest from elbow to elbow, and estimated the depth of the coffin. Then with pencil and ruler he made drawings of the various parts and marked down the measurements in the proper places on the pieces of material. Tough, fine-grained pine boards were always selected. These were planed smooth and properly shaped by means of the saw and drawing knife. When the job was finished, no one could well mistake his handiwork for anything else but a coffin. Several yards of cheap, black cotton cloth and dozens of coffin tacks, with enormous, ornate, silver heads, were bought at the store. The cloth was fitted on the outside of the coffin and held in place by the tacks. What small boy would ever forget the gruesome effect of those silver tacks on that black background? The inside of the coffin was lined with cotton batting covered with cheap, white cotton cloth from the store.

In digging a grave for an adult, a rectangular excavation six feet wide and ten feet long was made. When the depth of four feet was reached, the bottom was smoothed and leveled off. Then a secondary excavation three feet wide and seven feet long and eighteen inches deep, called the vault, was made in the middle of the bottom. Into this vault a rough box made of heavy boards was fitted.

The coffin with the body inside was hauled in an ordinary farm wagon from the home of the deceased to the church. No attempt was made to form a funeral procession, but custom decreed that the mourners should ride in buggies close in the wake of the improvised hearse. At church the coffin was placed on two chairs in front of the pulpit, a chair at each end, and the lid was unscrewed and removed. Hymns were sung, a prayer was offered, and a brief talk was made by a preacher, usually the pastor of the church. Then came the exciting part, the part for which the small fry in the congregation had long been waiting, namely, the invitation to pass around the bier and view the remains of the departed for the last time. There was no unseemly rush, but all present took a long peek; even very young children, who could not possibly know what it was all about, were held up in the arms of their parents for a good view. The final scene was staged by the mourners, who bent over the pale clod of clay in the coffin and wept vociferously.

At the grave the coffin was lowered into the vault by means of a pair of strong, leather reins detached from some farmer's harness for the purpose. The task was not easy when the body was heavy, and was sometimes bungled. Once in the vault, the coffin was covered with wide rough boards, four feet long, laid crosswise. Then a tall, strong man eased himself into the grave and, reaching out with a shovel to the ugly bank of red clay, covered the bottom with a thick layer.

There was a lugubrious, hollow sound each time a shovelful of dirt fell on the rough boards. Emerging when the boards were well covered, the first shoveler was joined by a half a dozen others who hastily filled the grave to overflowing. The finishing touch was the construction of an impressive mound of clay running the length of the grave and tapering off to the level of the ground at each end. The tombstones were two long, flat rocks picked up in the neighborhood.

Graves were always dug with careful reference to the points of the compass — the head toward the west, so that on the Resurrection Morning the body would rise with the face toward the break of day and the rising sun.

If the deceased was a prominent citizen of the community or the wife of a prominent citizen, a regular funeral sermon was in order; but such a sermon was not preached for weeks and often months after the burial. Meanwhile the surviving partner of the deceased was expected to abstain from showing any signs of a disposition to make other matrimonial arrangements. A widow, for instance, disgraced herself in the eyes of her friends if she received any attentions at all from the sterner sex before the funeral of her late lamented.

Many people, particularly the very old and those afflicted with lingering, incurable diseases, selected the preacher and arranged all the details of their funerals years before they died, even to the designation of the place where the sermon was to be preached, the text of Scripture from which it was to be preached, the songs to be sung and the singers who were to sing them. Often life secrets were revealed to the selected preacher, religious experiences were related to him, and messages and exhortations were entrusted to his keeping for delivery in the funeral sermon.

People for miles around were attracted to funeral sermons. All were eager to hear the dying confessions and the last messages of the departed and to learn for certain what was the fate of his soul. The preacher, who had all the inside information and spoke as the Spirit of God gave him utterance, was expected not only to tell the congregation where the soul of the departed had gone but also to explain why it had gone there.

By Primitive Baptists the doctrine was firmly held that a certain number of human beings had been predestined to eternal damnation before the world was created, and that the number to be saved and the number to be lost were both so definitely fixed that neither could be increased or diminished. Moreover, it was generally understood that the number elected to salvation was exceedingly small. And yet, when a Primitive Baptist preached a funeral sermon, he always managed to place the soul of the departed brother or sister among the elect. Thereupon everybody went home well pleased with the result, except possibly a few personal enemies of the deceased who went away doubting that the judgment rendered in the funeral sermon would be confirmed by the upper court.

RURAL SCHOOLS

 IT WAS NOT DIFFICULT in the eighteen eighties and nineties to get a license to teach school in Clay County, Alabama. On the day appointed for the purpose the prospective teacher, usually a man, repaired to Ashland, the county seat, and took an examination prepared, supervised, and graded by the County Superintendent of Education, an official elected by popular vote. For a dozen years or more in succession the County Superintendent was A. S. Stockdale. "Col." Stockdale was not a teacher himself, but a mediocre lawyer and smooth politician, who knew how to keep himself in office by currying favor with the voters. Readily, on payment of the legally established fee, he handed out first grade, second grade, and third grade certificates by virtue of the authority in him vested by law and the tacit consent of the Board of Education.

After getting his license, the prospective teacher visited a community in need of a teacher and made a canvass of the situation. To each patron of the school he presented written articles of agreement stipulating the length of the term, the

amount of his salary, and other conditions.   Presently a meeting of the trustees and patrons was held at the schoolhouse
to discuss and possibly to ratify the articles of agreement.

Usually the most serious problem was financial.   How
much of the public funds could be counted on for this school
for the coming year?   How much could be raised by sub-
scription?

In the end, the candidate for the teaching job would probably be employed to teach a seven months school, beginning
in November, for the sum, say, of $280.   Since the school
could hardly expect more than, say, $70 from the public
funds, $210 would have to be raised by subscription.   The
newly appointed teacher was expected, of course, to make
the rounds of the community and collect the necessary
pledges.

No law had ever been passed establishing a uniform
system of textbooks for the public schools of the state, but
what the legislature had failed to do had been done, to all
intents and purposes, by custom and tradition.   In the schools
of Clay County the basic textbooks were Webster's *Blue Back
Speller* and *McGuffey's Readers*.

The first task of the beginning pupil was to learn the
letters of the alphabet which were printed for his convenience
on page 15 of the *Speller*.   In the first two columns of the
page were the Roman letters, small and capital; in the third
and fourth columns were the Italic letters, small and capital;
in the fifth column were the names of the letters spelled out,
thus: *a, be, ce, de, e, ef, je, aytch,* and so on down to *wi* and
ze. On page 16 were the Old English letters, small and cap-

ital; the letters in script, small and capital; and the arabic numerals in script. Fortunately the pupil was seldom required to learn much more than the Roman letters.

After the alphabet came the syllabarium which contained tables of nonsense syllables, two letters in length, such as: *ba, be, bi, bo, bu*. The pupil, with his eyes on the page and his index finger properly pointed, spelled each of these syllables orally and pronounced it. Then followed tables of three-letter syllables, such as: *bla, ble, bli, blo, blu*, and then tables of easy one-syllable words, such as: *bog, log, dog,* or *edge, wedge, hedge*. It was a proud day when the pupil reached two-syllable words, such as: *baker, shady, lady*.

Thus the pupil advanced from syllables to easy words, and from easy words to words that progressively became harder until he reached words of many syllables. Never was he allowed to forget that words are composed of syllables. When spelling a word of more than one syllable, he was required to pronounce each syllable when the spelling of that syllable was completed, then, dropping back, to pronounce the syllables spelled thus far, and, when the last syllable was spelled and pronounced, to bring his chant to a conclusion by pronouncing the entire word. Thus: I-N in, C-O-M com, incom, P-R-E pre, incompre, H-E-N hen, incomprehen, S-I si, incomprehensi, B-I-L bil, incomprehensibil, I i, incomprehensibili, T-Y ti, incomprehensibility.

Seldom did it happen that a pupil knew the meaning of a single word in his spelling lesson. But that did not matter. What do you want to know the meaning of words for?

Ordinarily during the first year of school the pupil had

no other textbook than the *Blue Back Speller*. When he had spelled his way as far as *baker* on page 25, he was turned back to the syllabarium for a fresh start. On his second journey forward he probably advanced as far as *banquet* on page 34 before he was turned back for another fresh start. After his third fresh start he probably made his way as far as *luminary* on page 51 before he was again turned back. By this time he was eight years old and ready for *McGuffey's First Reader*. But he kept his spelling book and continued for two or three years more, if indeed he remained in school that long, to advance and retreat over its difficult pages, until he reached *cachexy* and *chalybeate* on page 124 and at long last the pictures and fables at the end of the book.

McGuffey's Readers were an improvement over the *Blue Back Speller* in that they were designed to combine the word method with the phonic method in teaching reading. The pupil was encouraged to recognize simple words or groups of words at first glance, but if he encountered a word which he did not recognize immediately he was required to spell and pronounce it before going on to the next word. In the first lessons of the *First Reader* words of only two or three letters were used. Gradually longer and more difficult ones were introduced as the pupil gained aptness in the mastery of words. At the head of each lesson was a list of words that had not been used in previous lessons. These new words were to be spelled, pronounced, and rendered thoroughly familiar before the lesson for the day was read. The carefully chosen pictures that accompanied the lessons were designed to arouse the interest of the pupil.

It was customary for the pupil to read and spell his way through each of the *McGuffey Readers* at least three times before going on to the next. The first lesson of the *First Reader* was ridiculously simple for a child of eight. There was the picture of a running dog. Beneath the picture were the words: "The dog. The dog ran." But the last lesson on page 94 was at the intellectual level of a child of ten. The *Second Reader* was pitched at about the level of the fifth or sixth grade of our present day elementary schools. The *Third Reader* was designed for boys and girls who today would be ready for junior high. Few pupils in the rural schools of Clay County ever studied the *Fourth Reader*.

To McGuffey the development of moral character seemed as important as learning to read. His *Readers* were therefore designed not only to teach boys and girls to read but also to teach them the fundamental virtues necessary to right living in a good community. The lessons consisted for the most part of interesting stories which emphasized the moral value of promptness, goodness, kindness, honesty, thrift, truthfulness, reverence, piety, patriotism, and so forth. Many an elderly person today, and I include myself, can testify to the influence of these *Readers* in shaping character.

When a pupil had proved himself proficient in reading, he was introduced to the study of geography, grammar, and arithmetic.

Elementary geography was largely a description of the earth's surface and of the manners, customs, and occupations of the various peoples who inhabit the earth. The pupil was expected to read the lesson assigned for the day and answer the printed questions that appeared at the end thereof. Excellent maps accompanied the lessons, and part of the requirement was to locate cities, political boundaries, and natural features on the map. Most of the boys and girls found this exercise good fun: it was like hunting big game in Darkest Africa. As was proper, most of the textbook was devoted to North America, and particularly the United States; but South America, Europe, Asia, and Africa were not neglected. Numerous pictures showed natural scenery, animals, and conditions of life, and, through it all, there was a good deal of history to serve as background.

Grammar, like geography, was regarded as an advanced study. All the pages of the textbook bristled with definitions and rules which the pupil was expected to learn by heart. In the section devoted to etymology, parsing sentences and learning the conjugations and principal parts of verbs were the major sports. In the somewhat longer section devoted to syntax, the classification and analysis of sentences were the main preoccupations. In the Hatchet Creek community, grammar was not a favorite study. There were parents who said openly that they did not see the need of it.

Arithmetic, on the other hand, was a subject of which all the patrons of the rural schools recognized the practical value. Even before a pupil had completed the *Second Reader* he was usually introduced to Robinson's *Primary Arithmetic*. Here he learned how to write arabic numerals, how to use the plus and minus signs, the signs of multiplication and division and of equality, and how to perform simple arithmetical operations. Here also he was likely to have his initial encounter with the bar sinister to the study of arithmetic, namely, the multiplication table. This multiplication table had to be learned by heart, a task which required several sessions of school and much drilling on the part of the teacher.

Robinson's *Practical Arithmetic*, which was taken up by the pupil in his early teens and pursued during the rest of his academic career, was the principal study of the whole curriculum. In the popular mind the teacher's qualifications were measured by the deftness and dispatch with which he could solve the hardest problems in this notable book, and the pupil's progress toward a practical education was measured by the number of pages which he covered. Parents' enthusiasm for the cause of education rose and fell with the degree of effectiveness with which arithmetic was taught in the school.

Problems in arithmetic were "figured out" on slates or on the blackboard.

Today the slate, with its soft stone pencil, has given way before the cheap scratch pad, but in the eighties and nineties it was the commonest article of the school child's equipment. The strongest argument against the use of the slate was hygienic. Fastidious teachers might show their pupils how to erase writing with a damp cloth or sponge, but to school children this seemed a long-way-around method of achieving results that could be just as efficaciously attained by saliva and a brisk rubbing with hand or coat sleeve.

The blackboard was the handiwork of some local carpenter. It consisted of three wide boards, from ten to fifteen feet long, smoothly planed and painted black, and held in place, edge to edge, by "tongue and groove" and by cross pieces which extended far enough on one edge to serve as legs. This clumsy contrivance, with its painted surface exposed to the room. was stood on its legs and leant against the wall in front of the recitation benches. Pupils wrote on the blackboard with chalk and used old rags and pieces of sheepskin for erasers.

It was with chalk and slate pencils that pupils learned to write. If a teacher should happen to be adept with his Spencerian pen, he might encourage his larger pupils to bring copybooks, pens, and inkstands to school and let him give them instruction in penmanship. But the initial enthusiasm was likely to wane quickly. The furniture of most rural schoolhouses, consisting, as it did, of long benches, like church pews, and rickety desks, made penmanship a difficult undertaking. The copybook was a quire of foolscap paper swathed for protection in a discarded newspaper; the steel pen which fitted snugly into its holder was easily ruined by unskillful handling or by an accidental drop, point downwards, to the floor; and the open inkstand was easily overturned by a careless gesture or the wobble of a rickety desk, to the detriment of desk, clothing, and the sweet disposition of all concerned. The overall result was that very few pupils ever learned to write with a pen.

No law of the state required parents to send their children to school. As a consequence, attendance was woefully irregular.

On the opening day, usually the second Monday in November, the teacher, usually a new one, was met at the schoolhouse by about a dozen small children. He made a record of their names and ages in a roll book which he had brought along for the purpose, looked over the dilapidated textbooks which they had brought in, found out as best he could by personal interviews how much schooling each pupil had already had, and made lesson assignments. Not infrequently pupils came without any textbooks at all, in which case the teacher made such arrangements as he could for the bookless to study with the pupils who had books. These preliminaries out of the way, the teacher, standing in front of the children with his back to the blackboard, delivered a sort of inaugural address or pep talk, in which he explained that, while he was not going to be "tight" in his discipline, he was certainly going to see to it that every pupil present studied hard and refrained from mischief. He sincerely hoped, he said, that during the entire school year he would never have to apply the rod to any of his pupils; but if occasion arose, he warned impressively, he would lay it on the backs of offenders with right good will; and, to emphasize the point, he went through the motion of delivering a vigorous flogging. On returning home at the end of the day the pupils told their parents how tight the new teacher was going to be, and the parents smiled their approval.

By the third week of school the number of pupils had possibly increased to twenty-five or thirty; after Christmas, to sixty or more, and a lady assistant had to be employed to take care of the smaller children. During January and February adult pupils, varying in age from eighteen to even twenty-five, showed up with their arithmetics, grammars, and dictionaries for more schooling and possibly for a little courting. In

March, attendance began to diminish rapidly as the older pupils dropped out to labor on the farm, and the lady assistant was no longer needed. At the end of April the teacher was ready to announce to the dozen or more small children who were still in attendance that the winter session of the school was over and that the summer session would open in July.

The school day was supposed to be eight hours long, but if the teacher extended or diminished the length somewhat nobody complained. Custom and tradition demanded that there be an hour's intermission at midday and a recess of thirty minutes in the middle of the morning and again in the middle of the afternoon. At the opening of the school day at eight o'clock in the morning and at the end of each play period the teacher rang a large hand bell to summon the pupils to "books." During books the teacher sat in a chair up front, with his back to the blackboard, and "heard lessons." From his point of vantage he could keep the entire school room under surveillance. The pupils who were reciting either stood in line or sat on long benches up front not far from, and facing, the teacher. The pupils who were not reciting were supposed to sit still, keep their eyes on their books, and maintain silence. But of course it was impossible to keep a roomful of restless, mischievous children quiet. Frequently the teacher had to interrupt his "lesson hearing" to administer reprimands and punishments to the imps in the back of the room. A teacher who could maintain his emotional balance under such circumstances was certainly worthy of his $40 a month and his salt besides.

The younger pupils (and these comprised the bulk of the

school) were given a rough and ready classification. The most elementary class was composed of youngsters who were just learning to spell "on the book." These recited four times a day in the *Blue Back Speller*. When summoned to class they stood in line facing the teacher and took turns at spelling "out loud" and pronouncing the words in the column assigned for the lesson. Then there was a more advanced group who were just learning to spell "by heart." When summoned to class they stood in line and, with their books closed, took turns at spelling orally and from memory the words pronounced by the teacher. Since this group was also beginning to read, it recited twice a day in the *Speller* and twice in the *First Reader*. In the reading classes at all levels there was a good deal of spelling on the book and by heart as a supplementary exercise.

But irregular attendance on the part of pupils played havoc with the teacher's efforts at satisfactory classification. For weeks after the opening of school pupils drifted in, either singly or by twos and threes, and had to be assigned lessons; and few of these late comers attended regularly after they had been enrolled. The result was that the teacher was constantly forming new classes in spelling and reading, holding back bright pupils until stragglers could catch up, and indeed giving a good deal of individual instruction to pupils who could not be classified. If the teacher was an old hand at the business, he did not worry too much, but simply let things drift. A pupil who did not attend regularly enough to be classified could easily be neglected without much danger of protest from either pupil or parents.

The school day always ended with a large spelling class made up of all the pupils who had acquired any proficiency in spelling by heart. The textbook was not the *Blue Back Speller*, as might be too readily supposed, but a small abridged edition of Webster's *Dictionary*, which the American Book Company put out to meet this particular need of the public schools. The daily assignment was usually two pages, which the pupils were supposed to study carefully before coming to class.

In this spelling class the pupils stood in line across the room, with their backs to the blackboard and the wall. One end of the line was designated as the head, the other as the foot. Standing in front of the class and beginning at the head, the teacher gave out the words of the lesson, a word to each pupil in turn, to be spelled by heart. If a pupil missed a word, the next in line tried it, and the next, down the line until someone hit upon the correct spelling, whereupon he "turned down" the misspellers, that is, he moved up and took his place in the line just above the first pupil who missed the word. The pupil who kept his position at the head of the class during the class period without missing a word marched proudly to the foot at the end of the class period, thus making a "head mark," a record of which the teacher pretended to keep in his roll book. If a pupil was absent from school one or more days, he lost his place in the line and had to "go foot" for a fresh start.

On many a Friday afternoon, particularly during the weeks when attendance was at its peak, the pupils importuned the teacher to devote the period after the last recess of the day to a "match spelling," and the teacher, fed up with the routine of hearing lessons, was usually ready to yield to the importunity.

The match spelling began with the designation by the teacher of two good spellers to choose up, that is, to take turns in choosing the spellers for each side. The question as to who should have the first choice was decided by catching a certain point in a tossed-up cane or guessing a page in a book. The spellers as they were chosen sprang enthusiastically from their seats and took their places in the two lines that stretched across the room facing each other. The teacher, standing between the lines, gave out the words, a word to one side and a word to the other, and continued to do so until all the spellers on one side were spelled down. The side that still had spellers standing was declared the winner.

The book from which the teacher gave out the words in a match spelling was usually the *Blue Back Speller,* because the pupils were more familiar with that book than they were with Webster's small abridged dictionary. After having spelled over the pages of the old *Blue Back* a dozen times or more, both "on the book" and "by heart," the brightest of the pupils could spell *erysipelas, asafetida,* and even *caoutchouc* correctly without batting an eye.

In none of the rural schools of Clay County were there adequate tests, either oral or written, to determine the degree of progress made by the pupils; but at the end of the two months' summer session it was the usual practice (if the teacher was not too bored with his job or too unpopular in the community) to devote the last day of school to an Examination and the evening thereof to an Exhibition. On the day appointed, parents of the children and friends of the school flocked in from the entire neighborhood and spent the day at the schoolhouse and its environs in a sort of picnic atmosphere. There was even likely to be a lemonade stand on the grounds where one could buy that beverage for five cents a glass. The exercise began around ten o'clock in the morning and took the form of a series of recitations by the pupils, recitations which had been carefully rehearsed for this particular occasion. At noon there was a two hour intermission when a sumptuous free dinner was served on the grounds. In the afternoon came recitations in arithmetic. Young children showed on the blackboard how well they could add, subtract, multiply and divide; older pupils showed how deftly they could solve problems in fractions and in percentage. Occasionally members of the audience asked questions or submitted problems to be solved. At four or five o'clock the Examination was brought to a close by a spelling match, in which any boy or girl who had been in the school during the year was privileged to take part. Then on invitation from the teacher, "distinguished visitors" from the audience made brief talks, in which they praised the teacher for the excellent showing made by his pupils.

In the evening at seven o'clock the audience was back in the school room to witness the Exhibition. For this performance the pupils had been carefully trained by the teacher. They sang songs, engaged in dialogues, enacted short plays, performed stunts, and displayed their ability to "declaim" and "recite." One of the most popular declamations began as follows: "Friends, Romans, countrymen, lend me your ears!" Some of the bigger boys could really make the welkin ring with their pompous oratory. The girls recited "pieces," such as "Curfew shall not ring tonight." The audience was always sympathetic and sometimes enthusiastic. Oil lamps brought from neighboring homes and lightwood (pronounced litered) torches furnished the illumination.

There would be no more school until November, when, in all probability, there would be a new teacher.

MY EXPERIENCE AS A

SCHOOL BOY

 IN THE SUMMER of 1887, when I was a little more than six years old, I accompanied my sister Eva to school. Since Eva was already nine years old, she was quite familiar with the rules and customs of school life and well acquainted with the other children whom we found there. But I was shy and taken aback at the strangeness of it all. At first I clung to Eva and insisted on sitting by her side. This behavior on my part attracted the attention of the other children, who kept looking at me and snickering. At the morning recess several small boys made overtures of friendship to me and said in effect: "Come over and sit with us; boys don't sit over there with the girls." Their friendly attitude won my confidence, and I moved over to their benches. They explained to me that I must not talk out loud during books, but only whisper. Soon I felt thoroughly at home.

The schoolhouse stood beside the Goodwater-Talladega road, on the public domain, only a few steps from Shiloh Church. It was an old dilapidated structure, consisting of only one room, with a large rock chimney and fireplace at one end. The end where the chimney stood rested on the ground; the other end, where the door and doorsteps were, rested on pillars three or four feet above the ground. When school was not in session, hogs and goats, and possibly sheep, found shelter and sleeping quarters under the floor during inclement weather.

There was an aisle between the door and the fireplace. At right angles to the aisle stood the backless benches for the pupils. In the corner to the left, as one faced the fireplace, was a small box-like, homemade desk, with a sloping top, for the teacher, and a heavy, straight-backed chair.

My first teacher was John Towles, a stocky man about fifty years old. He wore a bristly mustache which came straight down over his lip, and an enormous gold watch chain. The mustache was discolored with tobacco juice, and there was about his clothes and breath the vile odor of a pipe. He spent most of his time sitting, with his chair leant against the wall midway between the desk and the fireplace. Over his head, resting on two nails partway driven into the wall, was a smooth hickory switch a yard long.

The beginners, that is, the "a-b-c class," were summoned one at a time to say their lessons. When summoned, the pupil came with his *Blue Back Speller* open at the alphabet and took his stand close beside the teacher. With his pencil Mr. Towles pointed to each letter in turn, beginning at the top of the column, and called it by name and the pupil pronounced the name after him. When the last letter at the bottom of the column was reached, Mr. Towles pointed to a queer little curlicue off a little to one side and, in a jolly tone and with a twinkle in his eye, said *ampersand,* and the pupil, imitating the tone, also said *ampersand.* Thereupon both teacher and pupil laughed a jolly laugh and started back up the column pronouncing the letters in reverse order.

During the entire summer session, four times a day, I stood beside Mr. Towles and repeated after him the letters of the alphabet. I acquired self-confidence, spoke out loud, and tried to attract the attention of other children to my performance. But I did not not learn to spell "on the book." The only character I learned to recognize on the printed page was *ampersand* which, as Mr. Towles pointed out to me, looked like a little dog scratching his ear.

It can hardly be said that Mr. Towles was tight in his discipline. Usually he was good-natured and fatherly in his attitude towards his pupils. He even encouraged us small children, during the long summer afternoons, to stretch out on the backless benches for a nap. But one afternoon near the end of the session the storm broke. Mr. Towles, in what seemed like a towering rage, sprang from his chair, grabbed two of the bigger boys by their collars, dragged them up front, and gave them such a larruping with the seasoned hickory switch as I never hope to see again. The boys held up their arms to ward off the blows, danced about, and wept vociferously. Then as suddenly as it had arisen the storm subsided, and there was a great calm. The next day Mr. Towles was again his good-natured self, and so far as I know there were no repercussions from parents back home.

The summer session ended without the folderol of an

Examination or an Exhibition and Mr. Towles disappeared from the community and I never saw him again. For a year thereafter we had no school.

During the year when we had no school I somehow acquired the ability, possibly under the tutelage of my sister Eva, to say all the letters of the alphabet by heart, to spell on the book, and to read in the *First Reader*. When school started keeping again, in November, 1888, I was no longer in the a-b-c class.

My second teacher was Eli Horn, a youngish man of about thirty, with dark hair and a nice mustache that ended in little twists at the corners of his mouth. He never laid down any rules of conduct to be observed by his pupils; he never kept a hickory switch on display or said much about corporal punishment; but from the first days of school we pupils sensed that Mr. Horn was going to be tight in his discipline, and we stood somewhat in awe of him.

The schoolhouse now was not the old dilapidated structure where Mr. Towles had taught, but the Shiloh Church. The blackboard had been brought over and leant against a wall; the chair had been placed in front of the pulpit; the communion table was brought into requisition as the teacher's desk. The pupils sat on the hard, wooden, homemade, and thoroughly uncomfortable benches which on church days served the congregation as pews. These benches had backs indeed, but the backs were not so constructed as to be of much service to small children. From the seats small legs and feet dangled without being able to touch the floor. A large wood-burning stove, with its pipe running straight up through the ceiling and roof, stood in the center of the room. On chilly days pupils crowded around the stove to keep warm.

Mr. Horn's methods of instruction were in no way unusual. Twice a day I recited in the *Blue Back Speller,* standing in line with other children and spelling on the book, and twice a day I stood in line and took my turn at reading in *McGuffey's First Reader.* Before the summer session was over in August, 1889, I was spelling by heart.

The reputation of the school must have spread considerably, for half a dozen grown young men who habitually lived elsewhere came to board in the community in order to avail themselves of the educational advantages to be found there, and possibly to do a little courting.

Arithmetic was the principal study of all the adult pupils. With slate and slate pencil they spent the morning working problems in Robinson's *Practical Arithmetic;* at some time in the afternoon they were summoned for a recitation in that subject, and were sent to the blackboard to display their mathematical ability by solving and explaining problems selected by the teacher. There was no such thing as keeping together in an arithmetic class. Each pupil hoed his own row, so to speak, without reference to the progress made by others.

As the grand finale of each long school day, all the pupils who had acquired any proficiency in spelling by heart, were summoned to the big spelling class in the dictionary.

Mr. Horn had a flexible ruler a yard long, made of seasoned oak or hickory, and polished to a mirror-like smoothness, which he frequently carried in his hand as a sort of wand or pointer, or used as a straight-edge when he made

drawings on the blackboard. His crisp voice, raised in reprimand, was usually effective in keeping order in the school
room; but now and then he lifted a mischievous urchin from
his seat and applied the ruler with a vicious slap to his back-
side. The result always seemed to justify the means. Only
once, as I remember, did Mr. Horn administer a whipping
en règle. That morning as we came in for books, we found
him seated in his chair with a long hickory switch lying in
front of him on the communion table. Presently he called
up four boys and a girl, ranging in age from ten to twelve,
and talked to them for several minutes, while the school room
maintained a profound silence. Then with tears in his eyes
and in his voice, he picked up the switch, flexed it in his
hands, and laid it on the backs of the culprits with energy,
until all of them wept copiously. That performance increased
our respect for Mr. Horn and enhanced our awe of him.

The summer session of Mr. Horn's school closed with the
traditional Examination and Exhibition. To give a sense of
the color and flavor of the occasion, I will quote from two
contemporary accounts.

From the *Clay County Advance,* published at Ashland,
under date of September 13, 1889:

"Sure enough the closing exercises of Prof. E. Horn's school
was a success. It was not our good pleasure to be present in
the forenoon, but arrived in the evening [afternoon] in due
time to see the students examined in mathematics, which
showed that they had been properly instructed by their excellent teacher. At 4:30 o'clock p.m., there was an intermission of about two hours for the purpose of making
preparations for the exercise at night. The time arrived, which

was about 6:30, when the boys and girls began to walk out on the stage, and recited their pieces in a creditable manner, evincing the fact that they had been thoroughly trained in elocution. Millerville was well represented, and people from other parts too numerous to mention. Good order prevailed throughout the entire exercise, except with a few thoughtless boys.

From the *Central Democrat,* also published at Ashland, under date of September 26, 1899:

You ought to have been present at the examinations and concert at the close of Prof. E. L. Horn's school. Various parts of Clay were represented. If you could of heard the questions propounded by the teacher and others, and the ready answers given by the students, you would have been convinced that they had been well instructed by their excellent teacher.

My third teacher was Marshall Pitts, the son of Ma's oldest sister, Aunt Susan Pitts.

Cousin Marshall was a devout Methodist and an ardent advocate of temperance. On the first Monday morning in November, 1889, when we children gathered at Shiloh Church, which still served as the schoolhouse, we found on the four walls of the room a dozen or more cardboard placards bearing in large, black letters such mottoes as the following: "Remember the Sabbath Day to keep it holy"; "Remember now thy Creator in the days of thy youth"; "Lost time is never found"; "No idleness here"; and the like. When the bell rang for books we all took our seats on the hard pews and gazed with curiosity at our new teacher. After greeting us kindly and making a few appropriate remarks, he read to us a portion of

God's Word and offered a prayer. Then he enrolled our names and assigned lessons.

Each school day thereafter began with a brief devotional service. First, Cousin Marshall called on each pupil to repeat a verse of Scripture; then he opened the Bible and read us a portion of the Divine Word, commented on what he had read in the tone of a Sunday school teacher, and offered a prayer.

A few pupils from Methodist and Missionary Baptist homes, who had attended Sunday school, could, as it turned out, repeat Scripture verses with glibness, although the brief verse, "Jesus wept," was a bit overworked. But the children of Primitive Baptists were caught with their pantaloons down.

In his demand for verses Cousin Marshall was relentless and would not be content with just one verse repeated day after day. One night after supper my brother Elijah opened Pa's Testament and, after a diligent search, came up with a verse which he declared, with a mischievous grin, would just about fit my case. The verse read: "And Jesus, when he had found a young ass, sat thereon as it is written." Lijie helped me to commit the verse to memory, and the next morning I repeated it with gusto in the school room when my turn came. There was a snicker among the pupils, and Cousin Marshall looked at me suspiciously. When I repeated it again the next morning, he told me in a tone which I could not fail to understand that the time had come for me to learn a new one.

While teaching us spelling, reading, and arithmetic, Cousin Marshall found many opportunities to talk to us about the importance of religion, morality, and temperance. He would tell us boys how sinful it was to play marbles or ball, to go rabbit hunting or fishing or swimming, or to let our traps for birds remain setting, on Sunday. Impressively he would say to us at times: "You are never too young to die." Then he would urge us to think about religion, to read God's word, attend church and Sunday school, and possibly be baptized. "In church," he would say, "when prayer is being offered, you should bow your head and, with closed eyes, follow the words of the prayer with your ears and respond with your heart." He told us how wicked it was to swear and to use smutty words. And occasionally he would ask a class of boys and girls how many would promise never to touch liquor or use tobacco in any form.

This religious and moral instruction, spread over an entire school year, was not without its effect. As a small boy of eight, I began to give serious consideration to Cousin Marshall's suggestions.

On Friday afternoons it was Cousin Marshall's custom to devote the period after the last recess to a song service. He was no great singer himself; but fortunately we had in our midst a young man about twenty-five years old, named C. E. F. Smith, a boarding student, who had come from Delta, in the northeastern part of the county, to attend our school. Smith was a modest young man, with a pleasant singing voice and an elementary knowledge of music. In his vest pocket he carried a tuning fork which, when called on to lead the singing, he made use of to determine the proper pitch. From some source or other had come to us a supply of cheap song books. Under Smith's leadership we sang many songs that were already familiar, especially so to the boys and girls who had attended Sunday school, and we learned a few new ones. The favorites were: "O why not tonight?" "Bringing in the sheaves," and "Yield not to temptation." At the close of the service we always sang "God be with you till we meet again." All the pupils thoroughly enjoyed this break in the monotony of school routine, and most of them joined lustily in the singing.

Among other accomplishments, Cousin Marshall was an excellent penman. With a Spencerian pen he could draw beautiful swans, birds, and even human heads and faces; he could make capital letters with impressive flourishes and shadings; and his small letters were not one whit inferior to the script printed in the *Blue Back Speller* on page 16.

At the opening of the summer session, when the pupils no longer had to crowd around the stove to keep warm, he offered to give instructions in penmanship to pupils who would bring the necessary writing material to school. With hammer, nails, and pine boards, a writing table twelve or fifteen feet long and three or four feet wide was constructed and placed at one end of the room, and seats were arranged around it. Copy books, pens, and inkstands appeared on the scene, and the instruction began. Cousin Marshall showed us how to place our elbows and forearms on the table and grasping the pen loosely, to write without much, if any, finger movement. Our first exercise was to make a series of oblong circles slanting slightly to the right, by running our pen around and around, barely touching the paper.

At first there was great enthusiasm over the prospect of learning to write with a pen, and pupils spent a good deal of time at the writing table. For a while Cousin Marshall was kept busy inspecting copybooks and offering criticisms. But presently the enthusiasm waned. The initial exercises turned out to be boring; inkstands were accidentally overturned, pen points blunted, and copybooks blotted. Before the summer session was over, few, if any, were persisting in their efforts to learn to write with a pen.

I do not think Cousin Marshall ever switched any of his pupils. My impression is that he was opposed to corporal punishment for children. When a pupil misbehaved in school room or elsewhere, Cousin Marshall lectured him in a tone of deep moral earnestness and kept on lecturing until the culprit was thoroughly penitent and perhaps reduced to tears. There was some complaint from parents that the school room was too noisy and disorderly, but we pupils did not think so. Our feeling for our teacher was one of respect and even affection, unmixed with fear.

The closing days of the summer session were enlivened by the excitement incidental to the coaching and rehearsing for the traditional Examination and Exhibition.

My fourth teacher was J. C. Carmichael, a stanch Presbyterian, who had the distinction of holding the job for two years in succession. Mr. Joe, as the pupils soon called him, was about fifty years old, bewhiskered and baldheaded. Before becoming a teacher he was a farmer in the Brownville community five or six miles to the south of us.

When Mr. Joe became our teacher in November, 1890, we had a new schoolhouse, a frame structure in the form of a T, which stood on the site of the old one where Mr. Towles had taught. At the bottom of the T, facing the road, was a door; at the end of the left hand prong, facing the church, was another door; at the end of the right hand prong was a rock fireplace; in the center of the body of the T was a tall stove. Cumbersome, homemade desks, each to accommodate two pupils and their books, were arranged about the floor space. The girls were seated in the area about the fireplace, the boys near the stove. The long blackboard leant against the wall at the top of the T. The teacher sat behind a small table with his back to the blackboard, from which point of vantage he could survey the entire school room. Out in front of him facing the blackboard, were two long benches, exactly like the church pews across the way, for the accommodation of pupils who sat while they recited.

Without doubt Mr. Joe was a sincere Christian, but apparently he did not feel it his duty to emphasize religious instruction. He did not open school in the morning with Bible reading and prayer, nor did he bring the week's work to a close on Friday afternoon with a song service.

During the two years when I was a pupil under Mr. Joe's tutelage, I passed from childhood to obstreperous boyhood. I studied geography, grammar, and of course arithmetic. At the close of each school day I stood in the large, catch-all spelling class and took my turn at spelling by heart the words given out by the teacher. I was pretty good at spelling and occasionally made a "head mark."

Mr. Joe was kind and fatherly in his attitude toward his pupils, and not very strict in his discipline. But he must have kept a hickory switch handy somewhere in the school room, for I have a vivid memory of one occasion when the switch was suddenly put to vigorous use.

It was on a chilly day during books, when the boys were crowded around the stove to keep warm. My brother Warner and Drew Rozelle, both of whom were grown young men, were teasing me just for the fun of seeing me flare up in anger. Not finding it possible to retaliate in kind, I stood up and struck my brother Warner, who was seated, a resounding blow on the head with the flat of my slate. The slate broke into fragments, and there was considerable excitement around the stove. Mr. Joe appeared on the scene with a hickory switch and gave me a sound trouncing, the first I had ever received at the hands of a teacher.

I was deeply humiliated, especially when the other boys snickered and looked at me with gleams of joy in their eyes. To this day, more than sixty years later, I feel an injustice was done. I may have needed a licking on general principles — for being a smart alec and mischief maker, perhaps — but not for striking back at my adult tormentors, who deserved as much punishment as I did.

For the Exhibition at the end of the summer session in 1892, a temporary stage was built outside the schoolhouse at the door facing the church. The floor of the stage, which was two or three feet above ground, was made of rough boards insecurely tacked down on a trestle-like framework. One afternoon while rehearsals were in progress, and girls and boys were walking or standing about on the stage, an urchin named Albert Dison crawled under the floor and, peeping up through the cracks, caught glimpses of — feminine underwear! Albert emerged and, with great glee, passed the word around among his friends. Immediately there was a rush of small boys for advantageous positions in the peep show. But the alarm was soon sounded; exeunt all the girls and Mr. Joe, shocked and indignant, took matters firmly in hand. Inside the schoolhouse there followed a mass flogging in which three hickory switches were worn to frazzles. Some protecting divinity must have been hovering over my head that afternoon, for I was not one of the culprits.

Mr. Joe was succeeded by a young man named Greenberry Jenkins, who soon proved himself to be dull and incompetent as a teacher. Mr. Jenkins followed the traditional routine of hearing lessons, but he lacked the ability to enliven or inspire. Whereas all the other teachers before him had frequently stood up in the school room from time to time and, in a friendly, easy manner, made little talks to the pupils, Mr. Jenkins could not even make brief announcements without trying to cover up his shyness with a cloak of crabbedness. As a result, the pupils soon came to look upon him as something to be endured, but not greatly respected.

Mr. Jenkin's stock really took a tumble after Christmas, when the older pupils began to return to school with their *Practical Arithmetics*. Mr. Jenkins tried hard enough, but he simply could not solve the problems that lay beyond the middle of the book. When this fact was realized, the older pupils began to drop out of school, and the teacher's prestige dropped to nadir. What was the use of going to school at all if your teacher could not help you with your arithmetic?

Mr. Jenkins finished the school year, but only the younger

children stayed with him. At the close of the summer session he made no attempt to have the traditional Examination and Exhibition.

The quest was now for a competent teacher, and the choice fell on Silas Horn.

Si Horn, in his early twenties, had for a few weeks assisted his brother Eli when the latter taught in the Shiloh Church, and had distinguished himself at the time by his manly bearing, his impressive voice and manner, and his firmness of character. Already he was known as the bright young man of Horn's Valley. All his friends were justly proud of him, and he was frequently called on for public addresses at picnics and other gatherings.

Mr. Si Horn came to us in November, 1893, and proved to be a competent teacher, but perhaps too much was expected of him. He could do arithmetic well enough; he could make pleasant talks to his pupils; but he failed to raise the prestige of the school as high as it had once been under his brother Eli. No boarders came from elsewhere to attend, and the adult young men and women of the community seem to have lost interest in school. Only the small fry "with shining morning faces" showed up.

During the summer session Mr. Horn, knowing that he would not be there the next year, seemed to relax and let matters drift, and the rumor got around that he was lazy. The school frazzled out in early September without the traditional Examination and Exhibition.

My last teacher in the community school was James L.

Ingram, a local boy, son of "Uncle Monk" Ingram, and a cousin of mine by marriage.

Cousin Jim had many fine qualities as a man and was not incompetent as a teacher, but his reputation suffered from what is so well expressed by a verse in the Bible: "A prophet is not without honor save in his own country."

A few days prior to the close of Cousin Jim's winter session we received a challenge to a match spelling in the *Blue Back Speller* from Mr. Si. Horn's school in Horn's Valley. The conditions laid down were to the effect that all pupils who had been in attendance during the winter session were eligible to participate in the contest, and that side which spelled down its opponent twice out of three possible attempts would be declared the winner.

The contest took place on a Friday afternoon at our schoolhouse. From Horn's Valley came a long train of buggies and wagons bearing some fifty pupils and many interested observers. The moment the invaders arrived we caught a vision of the handwriting on the wall. Mr. Horn's school was bigger than ours and the average age of the pupils higher. We earnestly protested to Cousin Jim that he demand the exclusion of certain adults who looked especially venerable. But no: the articles of agreement had to be complied with. So we braced ourselves and defended the Pass of Thermopylae as best we could, but we were overwhelmed by the invaders. Twice in succession we were spelled down. There was no need for a third trial.

After the smoke of battle had cleared away, there were gestures of peace and friendship from both sides. The two teachers made pleasant little talks in which they complimented each other for having such a fine school.

I did not attend the summer session of Cousin Jim's school. Pa needed me at home to help him split rails, pull fodder, and make sorghum. The prospect was that I would never attend school again. I had studied geography and grammar and had worked my way through Robinson's *Practical Arithmetic*. I could spell by heart such words as *ecstasy* and *hegemony*. Here, certainly, was enough education for a farmer.

CHURCHES AND
RELIGIOUS PRACTICES

THE HATCHET CREEK community boasted three churches: the Primitive Baptist, the Missionary Baptist, and the Methodist. Since Pa was a Primitive Baptist preacher, I happen to know more about that denomination than I know about the others.

The Primitive Baptists were popularly known as Hardshells because of their harsh, Calvinistic creed. They believed King James's Version of the Bible "from kivver to kivver"; they believed that before the world was created God elected certain souls to be saved and condemned the souls of the rest of mankind to eternal punishment; they believed in baptism by immersion, and that baptism washed original sin from the souls of the elect, but not from the souls of the non-elect; they believed in "close communion," that is, that only those who had been baptized by an ordained Primitive Baptist preacher should be invited to partake of the Lord's Supper; they believed that certain men were "called of God" to preach the Gospel and were guided and inspired by the Holy Spirit while in the pulpit; they believed that "foot washing" was ordained by Christ and that the elect after partaking of the Lord's Supper should wash one another's feet; they believed in the resurrection of the dead and the final judgment. On the other hand, they did not believe in sending out missionaries to preach the Gospel to the sinner at home or to the heathen abroad; they did not believe in Sunday schools; they did not believe that their preachers should be educated; they would promptly excommunicate a brother who joined the Freemasons or any other secret society; they were also prompt to excommunicate a brother, be he preacher or layman, who was discovered to be "unsound" in his doctrine.

Our local Primitive Baptist Church was named Shiloh. The building was much like a country church of the present day, except that it was innocent of a steeple or any sort of paint. But the color was not altogether drab. Sun and rain had stained the pine weatherboards a dark brown. A door at each end and in the middle of one side gave access to the interior. The pulpit stood opposite the middle door. It was an imposing structure, this pulpit, being fully ten feet wide and as high as a man's chest, and its elevation was still further enhanced by the raised platform on which it stood. A bench on the platform back of the pulpit afforded seating space for the preachers, of whom there were at times three or four. An aisle connected the two end doors; another aisle led from the middle door to the open space in front of the pulpit where the communion table stood. Thus the wooden benches, or pews, on which the congregation sat were divided by aisles into four sections. In the section at the preacher's right sat the middle-aged and elderly men — "the amen corner"; in the section at the preacher's left sat the middle-aged and elderly women; in the two sections which more or less faced the pulpit sat the young unmarried people without segregation of sexes.

Religious services were held at Shiloh on the fourth Saturday and Sunday of each month. The Saturday service was usually attended only by the pastor and the stanch church members. Hymns were sung and a sermon was preached. At the conclusion of the Saturday sermon, which was usually brief and "uninspired," the members present went into conference for the discussion and disposal of matters of interest to the church. If one of the brethren had been seen intoxicated or heard swearing or been guilty of any other sinful or immoral conduct, or if he had been heard expounding unsound doctrine, the conference by a majority vote might prefer a charge against him and request him to come before the brethren and sisters in conference assembled and make a full confession of his guilt and a solemn promise to mend his ways. If the erring brother was indifferent to the request or proved to be obstinate, his brethren in the faith would go to him individually and privately and reason with him. If he still failed "to bring forth fruit meet for repentance," he would without many months of delay be excommunicated — "turned out of the church." And of course it was not impossible for sisters in the faith to be likewise disciplined for obstinacy in wrong-doing.

But disciplinary matters were not the sole concern of the Saturday conference. It was at this time that the doors of the church were opened for the reception of new members. When a candidate appeared, he was required to relate his experience of grace and submit to an interrogation by the brethren as to the genuineness of his conversion and the soundness of his doctrine. If he passed the test, as he usually did, he was admitted by a vote of the brethren to candidacy for baptism by immersion at the hands of an ordained Primitive Baptist minister.

These experiences of grace, however much they might differ as to details, always followed the same pattern: (1) For a long time my pleasures were in sin, vice, and immorality; but I intended to join the church some day and be baptized. (2) Eventually I began to have serious thoughts of death. How could I appear before God in my condition? A lonesome feeling came over me. I tried to pray, but could not. (3) Suddenly I felt a burden roll from my soul, and I found myself praising God. Now I know that I have been elected unto salvation, washed clean by the Blood of the Lamb, and sanctified by the Holy Spirit, and that I shall persevere in grace and never fall away.

The Sunday service was usually well attended. By ten o'clock people began to arrive in buggies, on horseback, and afoot. They hitched their mules and horses to trees and gathered in small groups here and there about the church grounds to talk and laugh. Young gentlemen and young ladies, dressed in their Sunday best, smiled at one another, and restless mules tethered to trees brayed at the sight of other mules. On the whole, the atmosphere was more social than religious.

At eleven o'clock singing was heard inside the church, and everybody went in and found a seat in the appropriate section of the pews. When quiet ensued, the preacher stood up in the pulpit, read two or three verses of a hymn, usually a familiar hymn, and asked the brethren and sisters to sing it. On the front seat of the amen corner, a brother, usually a deacon of the church, who was commonly regarded as a good singer, began to "hist" the tune. First he vocalized a bit in order to establish the proper pitch, and then he sang the first line of the hymn solo. When he reached the second line he stood up without pausing in his song, and the whole congregation stood up with him and joined in the singing. When the hymn was finished everybody sat down again.

The Primitive Baptist hymn book was a small volume, about five inches long, three inches wide, and an inch and a half thick, which contained the poetry but not the musical notes. At the top of each hymn, however, appeared "L. M.," "S. M.," or other initial capitals which indicated the meter. Easily, then, a good singer could pick the familiar tune that fitted the meter.

Copies of the hymn book were not numerous and were owned individually by stanch members of the church. On setting out for church on the fourth Sunday morning, a brother might remember to slip his hymn book into his coat pocket or carry it in his hand, but the chances were that he would forget to bring it along. The result was that at every service there was a great shortage of hymn books. In consequence the congregation had to sing by heart. The tunes of course were familiar but not so all the poetry. Out of this condition grew the practice of the preacher's "lining out" unfamiliar hymns. Here is the way it was done:

Preacher: "Amazing grace, how sweet the sound
            That saved a wretch like me."

Deacon sings the first line, rises while singing the second line, then pauses and waits.

Preacher: "I once was lost, but now I'm found,
            Was blind, but now I see."

Congregation, having risen with the deacon, sings these lines, then pauses and waits.

Preacher: " 'Twas grace that taught my heart to fear
            And grace my fears relieved."

Congregation sings, then pauses and waits.

Preacher: "How precious did that grace appear
            The hour I first believed."

Congregation sings, then pauses and waits.

Above the volume of sound could usually be distinguished the shrill voice of Miss Carrie Applewhite, an elderly spinster, singing "tribble." The effect was not always unpleasant, and might be soul stirring, depending on the enthusiasm of the moment.

When the hymn was finished and the congregation was again seated, the preacher either led in prayer himself or called on another preacher or a deacon to do so. Thereupon the stanch members of the church, including the sisters, turned in their seats and knelt on the floor, with their backs toward the pulpit. The young people, who were usually non-members, merely leaned forward in their seats and closed their eyes.

The prayer was always long, solemn, and labored. As it proceeded, brethren groaned deeply at intervals and sighed audibly: "God bless us!" "The Lord be merciful unto us!" When the prayer ended amid a chorus of "amens" from preachers, deacons, and others, the brethren and sisters resumed their seats and surreptitiously massaged their cramped muscles. Over in the amen corner, homemade spittoons were kicked around into convenient positions and preparations were made to relax and enjoy the sermon.

If two or three preachers were seated in the pulpit, as was often the case, there now followed a conference among them as to who should "take the stand" first. Agreement having been reached on that point, one of them stood up and stepped forward to the "book-board," or lectern. As he turned the pages of the Bible, he was likely to say that on his arrival at church that morning he had no notion of what he was going to preach about; but as he sat in the pulpit between Brother Harris and Brother Pruitt, listening to the singing and joining in the prayer, his mind kept turning to a certain portion of God's word which he would now read in the hearing of the congregation. Then he would read carefully and laboriously a familiar passage of Scripture, commenting as he went along, until his comments became a sermon. For ten or fifteen minutes he spoke slowly and haltingly, as odds and ends of ideas floated through his mind; but after a while his words came faster; the power of the Holy Spirit descended upon him; he drifted into a sort of chant:

It would be false and prideful-ah to take on a feelin'-ah that you can rescue yourself from the wrath of God-ah. Before

the ole world was built-ah God knowed-ah what was goin'
to happen-ah. He knowed-ah that Jesus Christ would save
as many as he could-ah from eternal torment-ah by sac-
rificin' himself on the cross-ah. An' God knowed-ah what ones
he was goin' to save-ah. He had 'em all picked out-ah ahead
of time-ah. All the rest-ah will spend eternity-ah bein' licked
by the flames of Hell-ah, damned to everlastin' perdition-ah
by the fall of Adam an' their own wickedness-ah. I tell you-
ah, brethren and sistern-ah, there ain't a feelin' in the world-ah
that kin make you feel so happy-ah as to find out-ah that you
are one of them-ah that God has picked out-ah to inherit
eternal bliss-ah. We're goin' to walk-ah with the saints-ah who
will never fall away or be lost-ah. On the Resurrection Day-ah
God's elected will stand on his right hand-ah and rejoice-ah
while the wicked shall groan forever-ah in the torturin' flames
of Hell-ah. Then us-ah that believe ever' word of the Bible-ah,
us that's been buried in baptism-ah accordin' to the only
right way-ah, us that knows the Lord's Supper-ah and washin'
of the saints' feet-ah was meant to be carried on-ah, us Primitive Baptists-ah, will stand-ah and see judgment pronounced-
ah on the dancin', card-playin' carnal sinners-ah, on them-ah
that read unscriptural works of men-ah, them that belong
to secret societies-ah when they ought to belong jest to God's
own picked and holy ones.[1]

The preacher's last dozen or so words would be spoken in
an ordinary conversational tone, leaving the distinct impression on the audience that the Holy Spirit had suddenly ceased
to operate. Then turning to the ministerial bench in the rear,
the preacher would ask Brother Harris or Brother Pruitt to

---

[1] This sermon has been lifted from Carl Carmer's *Stars Fell on Alabama,*
p. 61, and slightly modified, particularly by the addition of the "ahs,"
in order to make it conform to what I remember about Hardshell
sermons.

occupy the stand and take his turn at expounding the Gospel.

The rising and falling inflection of the preacher's voice during the chant — "the blessed tone," as it was popularly called — can not be adequately described, and will have to be left to the reader's imagination. The moment it became recognizable, the congregation would perk up and sit entranced, and brethren in the amen corner would catch the rhythm and chime in at the proper intervals with loud calls of encouragement. If several preachers were present, the service might continue for two hours or more.

Each Primitive Baptist church managed its own affairs without supervision of any sort from above, but annually each church sent delegates to an Association where matters of general interest were discussed and agreements reached, and where preachers vied with one another in expounding the Gospel from the pulpit. Shiloh was one of about twenty churches which belonged to the Hillabee Association.

In the early fall of 1892 the Hillabee Association met at Shiloh Church and remained in session for three days — Friday, Saturday, and Sunday. The church building was used by the delegates for their conferences; to accommodate preachers and their audiences, an "arbor" was built down near the spring. The arbor was a platform raised two or three feet above the ground and provided with a rustic pulpit constructed of rough poles and pine boards. Back of the pulpit was ample seating space for several preachers. A framework of poles supported a thick roof of leafy oak boughs to afford shade. The audience sat on rough benches, chairs, detached wagon seats, or the ground, or else stood about in groups.

The preaching began at eleven o'clock and lasted for at least two hours, several preachers taking turns at expounding the Gospel. Between one and two o'clock a bountiful repast was served under the trees on the grounds near the church, and everybody present was cordially invited to partake of the food. The afternoon was devoted to relaxation and social intercourse.

Accommodations for the night were provided in a rough and ready way by the Primitive Baptist families of the community. The delegates were assigned homes and treated with something like special consideration, but the throng of casual visitors from a distance found accommodation wherever possible or convenient. There were usually friends and acquaintances with whom one could spend the night; but, lacking these, one could ride up to any Primitive Baptist home and be welcome. Pa was widely known among the brethren and in consequence found himself the host to numerous guests. Saturday night was the most crowded.

In anticipation of numerous guests at the Association, Primitive Baptist families always prepared an abundance of food. Yearling calves and yearling goats were slaughtered and their carcasses divided among neighbors. Supplementing this fresh meat were huge platters of fried chicken, panfuls of hot biscuits, various sorts of pies and cakes, and what not. At the evening meal which was served at the home, guests ate in relays, beginning about five o'clock and continuing until about seven or eight. After the repast there would likely be a prayer meeting in the home, at which brethren related their religious experiences and some of them preached rather long sermons. On these occasions there was usually a considerable display of emotion. The meeting would break up with handshaking all around and tears and exhortations.

At bedtime the womenfolk, the delegates, and the brethren who were old and infirm found sleeping accommodations inside the house; the rest had to betake themselves to the cotton shed or the fodder loft with a few quilts to serve as covers.

The Association completed its work and disbanded on Sunday afternoon. The closing scene was emotional. Brethren, with tears streaming down their cheeks, shook hands with each other and "exhorted," while sisters wept and "shouted." The next day the Primitive Baptist families of the community washed their soiled dishes and cleaned up their premises and rejoiced that the excitement was over.

Each Association was divided into districts, so many churches to a district, and the annual meeting of the Association rotated among the districts. Each district, unless the Association was meeting within its borders that year, held an annual meeting of its own, to which member churches sent delegates for the transaction of business similar to that transacted by the Association.

The annual district meeting, invariably pronounced "deestrict" by the brethren, was the usual time for the communion service and the washing of feet.

Foot washing was a solemn and impressive ceremony. After the bread and wine had been partaken of, large tin basins, a supply of long towels, and pitchers or pails of water were brought forward. Simultaneously several brethren would stand up, lay aside their coats, gird themselves with towels, and pour water into basins. These brethren would then pair off with other brethren. Brother Jones would seat himself in a convenient place and remove his shoes and socks. Brother Smith, girt with a towel, would kneel at Brother Jones's feet, place the bare feet in the basin, slosh water on them, lift them out one at a time, and wipe them with the towel. Then the two brethren would exchange places, and Brother Jones would wash Brother Smith's feet. The ritual would be completed by a brotherly handshake, usually with deep emotion. Meantime the sisters would have paired off and washed each other's feet. For the protection of the Victorian modesty of the sisters, the front bench in their section of pews would be turned around, so that feminine ankles would not be exposed to public view.

At the conclusion of the communion and foot washing service the congregation stood up and sang an appropriate hymn, usually "Blest be the tie that binds," and then dispersed without the formality of the benediction. Did not the Bible say, at the conclusion of the account of the Lord's Supper, "And when they had sung an hymn they went out"?

Primitive Baptists did not believe in organized missionary efforts either for the conversion of sinners at home or for the salvation of the heathen in foreign lands, and they were scornful of theological seminaries for the training of pious young men to preach the Gospel. In 1886, when the Missionary Baptists of Alabama were making an intensive drive to raise funds for the support of Howard College, which had just been removed from Marion to Birmingham, the editor of *The Gospel Messenger,* a Primitive Baptist organ, wrote:

It would, indeed, be something new under the sun to find a record in the New Testament of the primitive churches sending out begging agents to solicit funds to establish, or endow, a Theological Seminary, in which "pious young men" could be prepared to preach the Gospel which is received not by man, nor taught to men save by the revelation of Jesus Christ. And it would be equally marvelous to find a description of the Honorable Faculty of such an institution — Directors, Presidents, Vice Presidents, Secretaries, Corresponding Secretaries, Treasurers and such like. How strangely would it sound to read in the New Testament of Rev. Paul, D.D., LL.D., President; Rev. Simon Peter, D.D., Vice President; Rev. Luke, M.D., Secretary; Rev. Simon the Sorcerer, Treasurer. And how would our astonishment increase if we should read in the New Testament of a Baptist State Convention as a great central institution of the Church of Christ, controlling, receiving, and disbursing missionary money, allowing no one to have a voice or membership therein, save upon a money qualification.

Nevertheless, there were Primitive Baptist evangelists, who, like the early Apostles, went forth in obedience to the command of Christ to preach the Gospel. They set out on their journeys with neither gold, nor silver, nor brass in their purses, nor scrip for the journey, neither two coats, neither shoes, nor yet staves, depending on the brethren of the faith for hospitality, transportation, and a little money to defray necessary expenses.

The most widely traveled and advertised of these evangelists in the late eighteen eighties was Elder J. H. Purifoy who had an humble home in south Alabama, somewhere in the region of Selma. Evidently he kept up a wide correspondence with the brethren of the faith and frequently received cordial invitations to visit Primitive Baptist communities and "fill the pulpit." These invitations he interpreted as a Macedonian call for help and, in imitation of the Apostle Paul, he set out, looking to the Lord for guidance and the brethren for support. On one of his missionary journeys he made a tour through faraway Texas.

When I saw Brother Purifoy, in the summer of 1889, he was around fifty years old. He had a dark complexion, black hair and long black whiskers, and must have weighed three hundred pounds. A glance at the picture of Leon Gambetta, the famous French politician and statesman in the early eighteen eighties, will afford some notion of his personal appearance. He had sent word ahead that he needed transportation, and my brother Elijah, then a young man in his early twenties, had gone with our family buggy to Mount Zion Church, a distance of twelve miles, and brought him to our house. When Lijie returned with the distinguished visitor sitting beside him, the top buggy, as I well remember, was listing dangerously to starboard.

Brother Purifoy spent the night at our house, preached the next day at Shiloh Church to a good congregation, and lingered in the community several days, enjoying the hospitality of the brethren before going on to his next appointment. Though he spent most of his time sitting, he was a delightful guest. He had a genuine affection for people, and everybody felt at ease in his presence. He talked to the menfolk about crops and domestic animals, he complimented the housewives on their cooking and neat housekeeping, and he was soon calling all the children by their first names. Before he left the community the good sisters of the faith had laundered his soiled linen and the brethren had surreptitiously handed him a few dimes and quarters. On the whole, it was not bad, this life of an evangelist.

To a greater or less degree, all Primitive Baptist preachers had ears that were sensitive to the Macedonian call, but most of them had family obligations that kept them within a short radius of home. Many of these minor evangelists came our way at times and preached at Shiloh Church, but I have a vivid remembrance of only one — Uncle Green Knight, who, with his long white whiskers, looked like one of the major prophets. When the power of the Holy Spirit descended upon Uncle Green in the pulpit, his rhapsody sounded like this: "In those days came John the Baptist-ah (hawk, spit), preaching in the wilderness of Judee-ah (hawk, spit) and saying-ah (hawk, spit), Repent ye-ah (hawk, spit), for the kingdom of Heaven is now at hand-ah (hawk, spit)." The hawking and spitting fitted in beautifully with the rhythm.

The Missionary Baptists[1] are so well known in the South that an explanation of their creed and organization seems unnecessary. In our community they had their Sunday school at Hatchet Creek Church every Sunday morning at ten o'clock and held their regular monthly meetings on the third Saturday and Sunday. They paid their pastor a stipulated salary and raised funds at times for the support of missions and other denominational enterprises.

[1] Missionary Baptists are, of course, the regular Baptists in the South. Nowadays the qualifying adjective is seldom used.

The exciting time at Hatchet Creek Church came in August of each year when a revival was staged which lasted for two weeks or more. Usually the pastor conducted the revival and was paid extra for the services.

At the revival in August, 1890, my brother Wilburn, nineteen years old, and my sister Eva, thirteen, offered themselves for membership. When Pa heard of what they had done, he was far from pleased. To Wilburn he said, "Go ahead; maybe you will mend your ways." But he thought Eva was much too young to know what she was doing. He called her into our parlor, closed the door, and proceeded to ask her searching questions about her experience of grace. All he got out of her was a flood of tears. In his quandary he searched his conscience and came up with a refusal to allow her to be baptized — at that time. There the matter rested. A dozen years later Eva joined the Missionary Baptist church in another community and gave August, 1890, as the date of her religious conversion.

The Methodists, who worshipped at Marvin's Chapel on the first Saturday and Sunday of each month, practiced infant baptism by sprinkling, admitted children to full membership in the church, and submitted to supervision by a bishop. In other respects they were not unlike the Missionary Baptists. They had their Sunday school; they paid their pastor a stipulated salary; they made contributions to missions and other denominational enterprises; and they had their annual revival at some convenient time during the summer months.

These three churches — the Primitive Baptist, the Missionary Baptist, and the Methodist — played a major role in the social life of the community. After a week of drudgery on the farm, a family, especially if it contained young people of courting age, was eager to get away from home for a few hours and to chat with friends. On a Sunday morning the mother saw to it that the small children were properly scrubbed and dressed; the grown daughter arranged her tresses, beautified her face, and robed herself in a long skirt and leg-o'-mutton sleeves; the grown sons shaved their chins, waxed their incipient mustaches, and put on their frock coats and derbies; and the father of the family, though not enthusiastic about leaving his easy chair, made some effort to look a little more presentable in his dress. The old double-seated buggy was rolled out for parents and small children, the newer top buggy for the grown daughter and one of her brothers, and saddles were girt on mules for the remaining brothers. Fully an hour before the religious services were scheduled to begin, people were arriving at church, gathering in small groups according to age and interests, and enjoying themselves. Young men and young ladies paired off and walked to the nearby spring or well for a drink of water (though in all probability they were not the least bit thirsty), lingered there for long moments to talk, and returned to sit together during the sermon. Even after the benediction was pronounced, people continued to linger about the church grounds to talk and beg friends to go home with them for Sunday dinner.

Church goers who lived near a church always expected dinner guests on church Sundays. Invitations were not considered absolutely necessary. Housewives prepared bountiful meals on those days and were disappointed if guests did not come and help enjoy the repast. At our home on the fourth Sunday, we seldom had fewer than a dozen guests of varying ages. At the first table service the middle-aged and elderly were invited to sit, with Pa at the head; at the second service, the young people; at the third, the children, with Ma and other mothers sitting with them or standing by to keep order. By the time the children were admitted to the festive board, the womenfolk were tired of washing dishes. So it frequently happened that ravenous children were served on plates that had already been used by dinner guests and merely scraped with knife or spoon.

By five o'clock in the afternoon the guests were departing, with loud expressions of appreciation for the hospitality enjoyed and with pressing invitations to come and see them at any time and especially to be their dinner guests on the Sundays when religious services were held in the churches near their homes. Such invitations were always accepted, and in due course the visit was returned.

SPORTS AND

OTHER AMUSEMENTS

 THE POPULAR SPORTS so widely advertised in the present day were unknown in the Hatchet Creek community in the days of my youth. I saw my first baseball game in 1895 at a picnic several miles from home. It was played by two teams hastily assembled after the crowd had arrived at the picnic grounds. There must have been some planning, however, for some of the players wore uniforms, and all used what we would now call regulation bats and balls. Measured by present day standards it was a poor exhibition of skill and sportsmanship. Players squabbled among themselves and with the umpire and shouted themselves hoarse. I do not think the game ever reached the ninth inning.

I saw tennis equipment for the first time in 1897, and even tried my hand at the game on an improvised court. I think it safe to say that none of us ever heard or dreamed of football before the turn of the century.

Such ball games as we knew about were played by boys (and sometimes by girls) at school. The ball was made of yarn raveled from a discarded sock; the bat was shaped like a paddle; indeed, we called it a paddle, never a bat. At the teacher's signal for the morning or the afternoon recess, we boys rushed pellmell from the school room with noise and clatter, sprinted for the paddles, and began the game of Paddle Cat.

In the game of Paddle Cat there were two bases located at a convenient distance, perhaps twenty steps, apart. On the bases stood the two batters facing each other. Behind each batter stood a catcher. Out in the field at various distances and in various directions from the batters stood such other players as elected to be in the game. The ball was tossed to one of the batters by whoever happened to have it. Thus the game began. If the batter missed the ball and it was caught by the catcher, even on the first bounce, the batter was out; the catcher took the paddle and the unsuccessful batter took the position of catcher. If, however, the batter hit the ball, the two batters exchanged bases, sprinting past each other. If the batted ball was caught by a fielder either on the fly or on the first bounce, the batter who had struck the ball was out and had to yield his paddle to the fielder who had caught the ball and go forth to try his own luck in the field. If the batted ball was not thus caught, but was allowed to bounce twice or roll on the ground, it might be picked up by a player and thrown at the sprinting batters. If one of the batters was struck or even touched by the thrown ball before he reached base, he was out and had to exchange places with the successful thrower. Since the ball was fairly soft to begin with, and became progressively softer from frequent use, it seldom inflicted pain when it struck a player. In nine cases out of ten the sprinting batter successfully evaded the flying missile and then shouted banter and ridicule at the unsuccessful hurler. After a ball had thus been thrown at a batter it was brought into play again by any player who picked it up and tossed it to one of the batters on the bases.

The game was fast, exciting, and noisy. In theory it might continue indefinitely, but in practice it was brought to a sudden end by the teacher's hand bell ringing for books. At the next recess it would be started afresh, when the two boys who ran the fastest and reached the discarded paddles first were "in" as the batters and the two boys who had run second best in the race were in as catchers. The other players, irrespective of numbers, took positions in the field.

At the noon intermission, which lasted an hour, Town Ball was frequently played. In this game there were two sides — we never called them teams — chosen by two boys, one of whom tossed up a paddle to be caught by the other in order to determine who should have the first choice of players. By the same process it was determined which side should be first at the bat or, as we said, in.

We never used such a highfalutin term as diamond, but there was a home base where the batter stood and there were three or four other bases arranged in a rough circle around the field. No basemen stood on these field bases to guard them, for, as will shortly appear, there was no need to protect them. The fielders scattered about and took such positions as appealed to their fancy.

The ball was pitched from a convenient place inside the

diamond by a player who was on the batter's side. Naturally
the pitcher took great pains to toss the ball in such a way that
the batter could hardly fail to hit it.   Behind the batter was
the catcher who belonged to the opposing side. If the batter
struck at a ball and missed it and the catcher caught it, even
on the first bounce, the batter was out and another player
from the batter's side took the paddle to try his luck.   If
the batter hit the ball, he undertook to run around the bases
and back home, being careful to touch each base with his foot
as he passed.   If the batted ball was caught by a fielder either
on the fly or on the first bounce, the batter was out and was
expected to go and sit down somewhere until his side was
ready to take its turn in the field.   If the batted ball was not
properly caught in the field, it might be picked up and thrown
at the batter as he sprinted between two bases.   If the
thrown ball struck or touched the runner while off base, he
was out.   Many a time a runner elected to stop at one of the
bases in order to escape serving as a target at close range, in
which case he was obliged by the rules to keep his foot on
the base until the ball was again tossed by the pitcher to a
batter.   It sometimes happened that two or more runners
were on bases.   If the ball was now safely batted into the
field and another runner added to the number on bases, two
runners might find themselves standing on the same base
with the fielder who held the ball standing between them
and the next empty base.   Since it was against the rules for
two runners to take refuge on the same base, the runner who
had reached that base first was called upon to admit that he
was out.   In response to this demand he usually called out

"Sheepin'! sheepin'! sheepin'!" which meant that he begged his adversary for a sporting chance. His petition was usually granted, and the fielder who held the ball stepped off ten paces at right angles to the runner's pathway and took his stance. Whereupon the runner took his chance, running, dodging, and writhing, in an effort to reach the empty base without being struck by the thrown ball. When all the play-ers on the side at the bat had, in one way or another, been put out, they took positions in the field and those who had been serving as fielders came in and took their turns at the bat. The game, in the parlance of the present day, had only one inning. The side which scored the greater number of home runs was of course the winner.

Not often, but occasionally, school boys played a rough and boisterous game called Bull Pen. In preparation for this game a large circle, perhaps fifteen steps in diameter, was marked off on the ground. Inside this circle a dozen or more boys ran around and shouted defiance at the two or three boys, each with a ball in his hand, who walked around out-side the circle picking out good targets. The object of the outsider was to deal a stinging blow to an insider and then escape retaliation by running away before the ball could be recovered inside the circle and thrown back at him. If the out-sider was struck or touched by a ball thrown by an insider, he had to exchange places with his assailant. The game usually ended in anger and fist fights.

In school also boys occasionally played Prisoners' Base, a game especially appropriate on chilly days. In this game there were two sides chosen as in Town Ball. Each side established a base at the root of a large tree, at a distance of perhaps fifty yards from the enemy base, and marked off a large circle on the ground nearby to serve as a prison. When preparations were completed, players on each side sallied forth from base and gave dares to opponents, that is, tempted opponents to pursue them. The dares were of course accepted, but with extreme caution, for the pursuer ran the risk of being intercepted and caught by an enemy player who had touched home base later than the pursuer had. In consequence there was much running forward in pursuit and running back to touch home base and running forward in pursuit again. If a pursuer fairly and legitimately caught an enemy player, he led his captive home in triumph and placed him inside the prison circle. But this prison camp had to be carefully guarded against invasion by enemy marauders. If an enemy player succeeded in breaking through the cordon of guards and touching one of the prisoners, he could lead his rescued buddy back to home base in triumph and thus free him for further service. The game ended when one side had caught and imprisoned all the players on the opposing side.

In the good old summertime, both in school and out, marble games were popular. Since a marble game required only two, four, or possibly six participants, it could be played in the shade of a spreading tree at school, in the yard at home, or by loafers down at the mill.

There were two sorts of marble games, Taw and Euchre.

For the game of Taw a ring about a foot in diameter was marked off on the level ground. In this ring five large marbles called "men" were placed — four in the circumference, in

such a way as to form the corners of a square, and one in
the middle. At a distance of some five steps from the ring
a straight line was marked off on the ground. This was the
taw line. The players toed this line facing the ring, each
with a small marble called a taw in his hand. When his turn
came to shoot, the player closed his hand in such a way as
to hold the taw in the proper position with his index finger,
with his bent thumb behind it to serve as propeller. He
then raised his hand to the proper level, took aim at the
"middler" in the ring, and "fudged," that is, thrust his hand
suddenly and energetically forward, and simultaneously
thumped the taw vigorously with his thumb. If the taw
struck the middler and knocked it from the ring, that counted
"game." If the taw knocked a man from the circumference
of the ring, the player kept on shooting until he had either
knocked all the men from the ring or missed a shot. If, without missing a shot, he knocked all the men from the ring,
that counted game. If he missed a shot, he had to let his taw
lie exactly where it stopped and give the next player an opportunity to display his skill. After all the players had taken
their shots from the taw line, it was permissible for him who
had the next shot to shoot at his opponent's taw. If he struck
the taw, the opponent was "dead" and could not play again
until the game was finished by the surviving players. If a
taw stopped inside the ring during a game, the player who
shot the taw was "fat," which carried the same penalty as
being dead. Of course, if all the players on one side were thus
killed, the game ended there and then, with the surviving side
declared the winner, and the players assembled at the taw

line for a fresh start. Usually the game continued until all
the men had been knocked from the ring. The most fun could
be had from the game of Taw when four players participated,
two partners on each side.

For the game of Euchre a square, five feet or more on each
side, was marked off on the level ground. A large marble
called a "man" was placed at each corner, at the middle of
each side, and in the middle of the square. Most inaccurately
this square was called the "ring." To begin the game, a player
knelt with his taw near a corner man and tried to knock the
man from the ring and, at the same time, make his taw
carom and stop in a position from which he could easily knock
out another man. He could keep on shooting until he had
missed a shot. Then he pocketed the men that he had knocked out and gave the next player an opportunity to display his
skill.

In Euchre there was no such penalty as fat. Indeed, a
player tried to keep his taw operating inside the ring; but,
when shooting from that position, he had to "knucks," that is,
hold the knuckles of his shooting hand firmly on the ground
and use only his thumb as a propeller. If a player shot at and
hit the taw of an opponent, the latter was dead; but not definitely so. From his pocket the deceased might take out a
man which he had previously knocked out and replace it in
the ring, thereby gaining a new lease on life. The game ended
when the last of the nine men was knocked from the ring.
The side that had pocketed the greater number of men was
the victor.

In both Taw and Euchre there were numerous rules and

technical terms that had to be mastered by the novice. If, for instance, a player objected to any sly maneuver on the part of his opponent, he could cry out "Vence!" which stigmatized the maneuver as irregular. Thus, if a player, when his turn came to shoot, should pick up his taw and ease around in order to shoot from a more advantageous angle, he could be stopped by the cry of "Vence your roundance!" Another veto frequently heard was "Vence your fudging!"

In school there was never any supervised play. Children of those days were enterprising enough to learn to play ball and marbles without being coached by paid experts. [1]

In addition to games at school and elsewhere, the inhabitants of the community, particularly the male contingent, indulged at odd times in hunting and fishing, uninhibited by any such marks of civilization as game laws.

By the 1880's the fleet footed deer, unable any longer to find adequate coverage in the woodlands denuded of undergrowth, had disappeared; but the wild turkey could still be found by those who knew where to look. At break of day hunters concealed in brush arbors sometimes succeeded in luring turkeys within range of their guns by scraping small wooden boxes on their gun barrels in such a way as to produce a sound similar to the turkey's call; but a hunter using this

---

[1] As a footnote to this description of school games, I would mention a strange custom which prevailed in my youth and for which I can offer no rhyme or reason. It was this. A gay young man, either a resident of the community or a stranger, might pass the school ground while the children were at play and shout "School butter!" In real or feigned anger at this unpardonable insult the boys would pursue the offender, hurling rocks and imprecations at him.

device had to be on the lookout for the hungry catamount
which might creep upon him in the half light, expecting to
find, not a man, but a turkey. In the spring of 1889 Professor
Eli Horn brought a catamount down from the mountain and
placed it on display at the mill, and winged rumor brought
people from all parts of the community to see it. As reported in the *Clay County Advance,* the big cat measured
three feet high and five feet long.

Squirrels were numerous. The hibitat of the gray squirrel
was the swamplands of creeks and smaller streams, where it
subsisted on nuts and farmers' corn. In the piney woods of
the hills and the mountain could occasionally be found the
fox squirrel, which was much larger than the gray one and
had reddish fur and black stripes on its nose.

Men and boys hunted squirrels with rifles and shotguns.
The barrel of the rifle was long, thick and heavy, with a small
bore spirally grooved to impart rotation to the bullet; its
surface was not round but octagonal. The hunter carried his
ammunition in a rawhide shot pouch at his side, slung over his
shoulder by a leather strap. To be strictly in fashion, the outside of the shot pouch should be covered with the hair of the
animal, usually a coon or a goat, from the skin of which the
pouch had been made. Firmly attached by a cord at each
end, and swinging horizontally outside the pouch, was the
powder horn, which was indeed a small horn taken from the
head of a deceased cow and fashioned into a convenient
powder container. When the hunter desired to load his rifle,
he poured powder from the small end of the horn into a small
measuring cup with a spout, called the "charger," and thence

into the muzzle of the rifle. Then a cotton cloth, called "patching," carried in the shot pouch for the purpose, was spread over the muzzle; the lead bullet was pressed into the bore on top of the patching; a keen edged pocket knife sheared off the protruding cloth at the level of the muzzle; and the ramrod was drawn from its place in the thimbles beneath the barrel and used to drive the bullet home. The hunter then inspected the projecting tube at the butt end of the barrel to see that it contained the fine thread of powder required to touch off the charge, placed a percussion cap on the tube, and locked the hammer to prevent an accidental discharge of the loaded gun. When the rifle was properly adjusted for firing, a slight touch of the finger on the "hair trigger" brought the hammer down on the percussion cap and discharged the piece.

The shotgun was either single-barreled or double-barreled, each barrel being round and smooth, with a large, smooth bore. When the hunter desired to load his shotgun, he poured a charge of powder into the muzzle and rammed a tight wad of paper down the bore on top of the powder and tamped the wad down snugly with numerous strokes of the ramrod. Then he poured in a charge of shot which was held in place by a loosely packed wad of paper rammed down the bore. After an inspection of the priming, the hunter placed a percussion cap on the tube and let the hammer down gently to rest on the cap. To fire the piece, the hammer was raised and cocked, aim was taken at the target, and the trigger pulled.

In my youth the squirrel rifle was already looked upon as

antiquated, but old timers still preferred it to the shotgun. A squirrel lying flat on a high limb, with only an eye and an ear dimly exposed, was safe from the flying pellets of the shotgun, but not from the bullet of the rifle. The old timer would prop his rifle against a nearby tree to steady his aim and touch the hair trigger; the bullet would graze the top of the limb just beneath the squirrel's belly and inflict a mortal wound. I have heard old timers boast that they seldom missed a shot with their trusty rifles.

Squirrel hunters usually went forth in small groups and took along dogs to tree the animals. When the barking of the dogs indicated that squirrels were nearby, the hunters spread out over the area and carefully searched the tree tops for the quarry.

Rabbit hunting appealed especially to boys. Flushed from its hiding place in the piney woods, the cottontail scampered away at a fast clip and, if pursued by a dog, usually took refuge in a hole under a clayroot or in a hollow tree or log, whence it could be dragged, possibly, by twisting a frazzled hickory withe into its fur. Swamp rabbits, flushed from hiding places by dogs, seldom took refuge in holes. Instead, they dodged about in the briers and underbrush, back tracked, and usually emerged after a while into the open field for a look-see. A rabbit squatting or loping along on the edge of an open field could easily be mowed down by the blast of a shotgun.

The season for hunting the shame-faced 'possum was autumn, when persimmons were ripe. This was a nocturnal sport in which firearms were not needed. The dog treed the 'possum up a 'simmon tree; the hunter either climbed the tree and dragged the 'possum down by his clammy tail or cut the tree down with an ax and let the dog worry the grinning animal on the ground until it "sulled," as we said—that is, pretended to be dead. When the excitement of the catch was over, a small pole was split, the 'possum's tail was inserted in the vise-like opening, and the pole and 'possum were carried away on the shoulder of the hunter. It was not unusual for a hunter to return home about midnight with several 'possums hanging from the same pole. Usually the animals were kept in the chicken coop a few days and fed roasting ears and scraps from the table. Ultimately they were taken from the coop and destroyed, for they were varmints. Seldom were they killed, dressed, cooked, and served as food.

Coon hunting was also a nocturnal sport, but too strenuous for small boys and weaklings; for coons, when chased by dogs, took refuge in the large trees of the swamplands and could seldom be dislodged. The young man who brought home a coon from the swamp had something to boast of.

Quail and turtle doves were numerous in the community and were hunted to some extent, mostly by adolescent boys with shotguns. The practice was to creep up on the sitting birds and fire before they took wing. The slaughter was never great.

The most effective way to take quail was to trap them in the wintertime when the birds were hungry. It was not unusual for a trap which had been well placed and cleverly baited to catch an entire covey of quail at one fell swoop.

For the quiet pleasures of the "compleat angler" the two creeks, Hatchet and Little Hatchet, each with its millpond and its numerous tributaries, furnished ample scope. The practice was to fish in certain places called "fish-holes," where the water was several feet deep and free from current. Familiar paths led through the underbrush to the fish-holes, and the bank adjacent to each was worn bare and smooth by frequent use. The hook was baited either with a fish-worm, local parlance for angle-worm, or with a minnow; a cork on the line was so adjusted as to keep the baited hook dangling an inch from the bottom; and the pole, a species of bamboo cut from the cane-brake, was either held in the fisherman's hand or securely anchored by inserting the butt end deeply into the soft earth of the creek bank. When the cork bobbed on the surface of the water, the fisherman knew that he was getting a nibble and became alert; when the cork was dragged under, he gave the pole a quick, upward jerk, hooked the unfortunate fish, lifted the wriggling creature into the air and brought it ashore.

The fishes common to the streams of the locality were: a species of minnow, popularly called "spot-tail," which was useful only as bait for trout and other cannibalistic fish; the sun-perch which might grow to be as wide as a man's extended hand and seven or eight inches long; a species of trout which might grow to be ten inches or even a foot long and might weigh a pound or more; a species of bass, popularly called "goggle-eyed perch"; a species of pickerel, popularly called "jack-fish," which had a long beak and spiny teeth; the sucker; the mud-cat; and the eel.

When fishing for trout, goggle-eyed perch, or jack-fish, the fisherman baited his hook with a minnow; when fishing for minnows, sun-perch, or mud-cat, he baited his hook with a fishworm; when fishing for suckers, he found it profitable to make preliminary preparations. First he "baited" a small area in a fish-hole with fragments of corn pone cast upon the water and allowed to sink to the bottom. After allowing several days for suckers to be attracted to this feeding ground, he baited the sharp point of his hook with a pea-sized ball of corn bread into which cotton fibers had been kneaded to give the ball cohesion and keep it from instantly dissolving in the water. With its thick, fleshy lips the sucker sucked at the bait; the fisherman was alerted by the slow bobbing of the cork on the surface of the water; a quick, upward jerk of the pole and a considerable tug usually landed the sucker on the shore. Early on a frosty morning was the best time to catch suckers.

The mud-cat was seldom caught except when the weather was rainy and the water in the streams quite muddy. To prepare this fish for cooking, it was first scalded to remove the skin.

Occasionally a fisherman caught an eel two or three feet long, on a hook baited with a worm. Usually he was highly elated at his stroke of luck and boasted to his friends of how the eel had pulled hard and nearly bent his pole double. The thin, tough skin of the eel was peeled off from head to tail in one piece, which then looked like a long, slender bag. Often it was stuffed with dry wheat bran and kept as a trophy. The flesh of the eel, when fried for eating, left something to be desired. There was a popular saying, of which, however, I can not vouch for the truth, that a piece of fried eel, if left uneaten till the next day, would be raw again.

The qualifications of a successful fisherman were laziness and an unconscionable degree of patience. The nervous person who kept raising his hook from the water to inspect the bait or kept moving from fish-hole to fish-hole in quest of better luck seldom caught anything.

For those who were too nervous to enjoy the quiet pleasures of the compleat angler, there was seining in the summertime.

As I remember, there were two seines in our community, a long one and a short one, either of which might be borrowed almost any Saturday afternoon by an enthusiastic group of young men and boys. The practice was to take the seine far down the creek and work back upstream until the milldam was reached. The fish-holes along the way were of course given particular attention. Stretching the seine across the stream and prodding the hiding places under the banks to scare out the fish, the seiners swept around in a wide movement and dragged their haul ashore at some convenient place, usually a low lying bank. This movement was repeated as often as it was deemed profitable. On reaching the milldam the seiners emerged from the stream, their clothes wet and muddy, and divided their catch. The next morning several families would enjoy fried fish for breakfast.

As boys of today learn to play baseball at an early age and regard inability to indulge in this sport as a mark of effeminacy, so the boys of my day and generation learned to swim.

On Saturday afternoon in the summertime, and on many a
Sunday as well, groups of small boys, clad in absolutely
nothing but sunbeams, might be seen swimming and heard
yelling in shallow pools at various places along the creek;
and stronger swimmers, both young and old, naked as God
made them, might be seen diving into the millpond from a
high springboard and racing about in the murky water. Bathing suits? Why cover up the handiwork of God? *Honi soit
qui mal y pense.*

COMMUNITY ACTIVITIES

 MOST OF THE TIME, life in the Hatchet Creek community sixty-five years ago was monotonous. Anything that tended to break the monotony was seized upon and exploited. Eyes lighted up with pleasure when a neighbor was observed passing by. You hailed him from your front porch and "passed compliments" with him; that is to say, you engaged him in something like the following dialogue:

"How're y'all?"

"Only toler'ble. The old woman grunts a right smart — pains in her jints."

Whereupon you allowed as how you were not feelin' very well yourself.

If the passer-by was in the mood to draw rein and tarry for further talk, you went out to the front gate and, leaning on the palings, carried on the conversation until a variety of topics had been covered.

On the Sundays when religious services were held in the churches, nearly everybody in the community put on bib and tucker and turned out, not only to listen to the sermon and the singing, but also to enjoy the society of friends and neighbors. Invitations to dinner were given and accepted, and a good time was had by all.

On many a Sunday afternoon, particularly in the summertime, people of the community gathered at one of the churches for a very zestful activity called a "singing." After crops were laid by, one Sunday at least during the summer was devoted to an all-day singing, with free dinner on the ground, to which people from miles around were attracted.

The music of these songfests was of two distinct brands, that of the *Sacred Harp* and that of the "seven shape notes." The twain were never mixed.

The *Sacred Harp* still has a dwindling number of devotees in the South, but I shall speak of it in the past tense because it was revised in 1911 and ceased to be exactly the song book that I knew in my youth.

The songs which it contained were, for the most part, melodies of England, Scotland, Ireland, and Wales, brought to our shores in the tenacious memories of our forefathers during colonial times and collected and published in the first edition of the *Sacred Harp* in 1844. Though the songs were religious, or at least tinged with religious sentiment, they were fundamentally folk songs and therefore not well fitted for incorporation in a church hymnal. Nevertheless, Primitive Baptists, though they never used the *Sacred Harp* in their church services, always placed the big oblong book of song next to the inspired Bible as the source of religious comfort and joy.

The music of the *Sacred Harp* was written in four notes: fa, sol, la, and mi, each with its individual shape. Fa was triangular, sol oval, la square, and mi diamond-shaped. Always before singing the words of a song, Sacred Harpers sang the notes, to make certain that the melody could be sung correctly before the sacred text was sung.

When engaged in singing, Sacred Harpers sat on benches forming three sides of a square. The leader stood in the middle. On the leader's right sat the basses, in front of him the tenors, on his left the trebles (pronounced "tribbles"). Tenor was sung by both men and women, treble usually by women only. A sizeable "class" might consist of a dozen basses, two dozen tenors, and half a dozen trebles.

In contrast with common usage in choral music, there was in the music of the *Sacred Harp* no definite tune-carrying part. The tenor in a measure performed this service, but the bass and the treble indulged in about as much running around and up and down as the tenor did. An urbanite of the present day, with his standardized musical background, would not be favorably impressed by this brand of music. He would be irked by the shrill voices of some of the singers, by the staccato or trotting movement of the songs, by the discords, by the dearth of melody or tune, and by the fact that all the songs sound pretty much alike.

Here we uncover the secret of the *Sacred Harp's* popularity: the songs were to be enjoyed by the singers, not necessarily by the audience.

Most of the songs were familiar to everybody and could therefore be sung by heart. When the leader, standing before the class, raised his arm and gave the down beat as the signal for the singing to begin, the response was a loud burst of sound. Drawing in deep breaths, the singers let out staccato yells. The arm of the leader, exact as a metronome, beat time; and the enthusiastic songsters, at full cry, kept on the beat. I have seen the Primitive Baptist Church in the Hatchet Creek community crowded on such occasions, people standing in the doorways, along the walls inside and around the open windows outside, all singing lustily. The basses rumbled, the tenors brayed at a high nasal pitch, and above all rose the screaming trebles. Beads of perspiration rolled down cheeks, but facial expressions were ecstatic.

Sacred Harpers normally learned to sing the songs of their beloved book from other Sacred Harpers and by constant practice, without the botheration of much formal instruction; but for teenage beginners, who needed encouragement and a little elementary knowledge of music, a ten day singing school was held at Shiloh Church nearly every summer after crops were laid by. The teacher of such a school was always a farmer, with limited education, who had acquired a considerable reputation in the community as a singer. To make up his school, he drafted a brief contract in which he specified the opening day, the length of the term, and the rate of tuition, and canvassed the community to determine the number of pupils that he was likely to have. If the number was sufficient to warrant the undertaking, the tidings were publicized and the school opened on the day specified.

On the morning of the opening day the teacher was met by twenty-five or thirty tuition paying pupils, who arrived on foot, in buggies, and possibly on horseback, bringing their lunches and song books with them. By nine o'clock the school was in session. After singing two or three familiar songs by way of creating the proper atmosphere, the teacher devoted an hour or more to formal instruction. On the blackboard he drew the four notes — fa, sol, la, mi — and drilled his pupils in running the scale. He showed them how to differentiate long notes from short notes; he showed them the marks that indicated "rest" and "repeat"; and he bade them look on their books and verify his instruction from observation. Then followed a recess for relaxation, after which the class divided tentatively into basses, tenors, and trebles. Songs were now sung, and occasional interruptions were made by the teacher to give further instruction.

In the afternoon the complexion of the class was changed considerably by the arrival of several experienced Sacred Harpers who came to participate in and enjoy the singing. These took seats among the tuition-paying pupils. The teacher was glad to welcome the visitors because they improved the quality of the singing and set examples for the novices to follow. So enthusiastic did the class now become that the singing continued with few interruptions until five.

Pretty much the same routine was followed on other days. The formal musical instruction never got beyond the most elementary stage, but the pupils learned to sing scores of songs, many of which were accounted difficult.

Although the teacher had little knowledge of music, he was expected to display two important accomplishments, namely, the ability to beat time vigorously with long sweeps of his right hand and arm, up and down, right and left, and the ability to sing any part in the song. Whenever the bass, tenor or treble lagged behind or broke down in performance he would rush to the support of the wavering or broken line and bring up the straggling forces. When any one of the parts got ahead of the others in performance, he would rush at the group that was singing too fast and burst into the unruly part of the song at the full power of his stentorian voice and swing his long right arm more vigorously than ever, to check the break-neck speed of the refractory warblers. By thus galloping around the sides of the square, he was able to keep all parts going and rarely failed to bring all in on the home stretch within a few measures of the same time.

On the last day of school the pupils, sitting on the front benches, and supported by many experienced singers on the back benches, gave an exhibition which lasted all day. After the school disbanded, the class continued to meet once a month on a Sunday afternoon, weather permitting, to keep in practice and possibly to improve their performance. The next summer there would probably be another "fa-so-la" singing school at Shiloh Church.

Devotees of the seven shape notes also had their singings on Sunday afternoons at either the Methodist or the Missionary Baptist Church, and likewise their singing schools in the summertime. But there was a difference in both the substance and the spirit of the performance. The seven noters had no sentimental attachment to any particular book. Indeed, they made it a practice to change books every year or so and thus keep up with the latest songs. Moreover, they could boast a little higher level of musical knowledge than the Sacred Harpers possessed.

The seven notes in question were do, re, mi, fa, so, la, ti, each with its individual shape. After a little practice in running the scale, a singer, given the pitch of a note to start with, could determine instantly the pitch of any other note in the scale by its shape. This simple device obviated the necessity of learning all that folderol about a, b, c, d, e, f, and g, which is such a stumbling block to beginners in their efforts to sing with nothing to guide them except round notes.

The music of the seven-shape-note variety was in four parts: bass, tenor, alto, and soprano. Soprano, which was definitely the tune-carrying part, was commonly sung by female voices.

Unlike the Sacred Harpers, the seven noters chose as the teacher of their singing school, if possible, a man who had studied vocal music under the direction of some famous teacher at some far-off place, like A. J. Showalter of Atlanta, Georgia, and who could display, printed in the new book which he proposed to introduce, a few melodies of his own composition. Such a man usually wore a necktie and was too distinguished to be called plain Mister; he was called Professor and treated with respect.

On the opening day of school the professor distributed copies of the new book among his pupils and stood ready to hand copies to all other interested persons. The price per copy ranged anywhere between fifty cents and one dollar. How much profit accrued to the professor from this transaction was of course never revealed.

Upon examination the new book would be found to bear some such title as *Prayer and Praise, Gospel Songs, Make*

Christ King, Worship of God, Christ is Lord, or some other catchy word combination indicative of the contents. Many of the songs were standard gospel hymns; but many were of recent origin, and some were entirely new. The tendency was to include songs of a light, joyous nature, which would be appropriate for Sunday school. Sacred Harpers frequently scoffed at such songs on the ground that they lacked substance and were sung moreover to sacrilegious "jig" tunes.

The school normally lasted ten days. During this brief period the professor usually managed to impart to his pupils a fair amount of elementary musical knowledge. He taught them to run the scale; he called attention to flats and sharps; he drilled them in singing semi-tones; he even explained the purpose and value of clefs. At the close of the school there was the customary all day exhibition, with free dinner on the ground for everybody, which was well attended and enjoyed by throngs of visitors. The scores of new songs which the pupils of the school, and other songsters as well, had learned to sing were thenceforth sung on Sunday mornings by Methodists and Missionary Baptists in their Sunday schools, at Sunday afternoon singings, at social gatherings of young people, and on other occasions. After a while, however, perhaps at the end of a year, the new songs began to grow stale and uninteresting, and the sentiment began to prevail that another singing school and a new song book were needed.

At singings and singing schools young people in particular had, or imagined they had, a great deal of fun; but the occasion *par excellence* for a good time by all, whether old or young, was the community picnic which took place nearly every summer. In the *Clay County Advocate*, under date of July 31, 1891, we have the following account by an eye witness of a picnic at Ingram's mill:

By 10 o'clock in the morning a good audience had gathered, and at eleven Mr. A. S. Horn,[1] a student from the State University, made a welcome address, followed by an address by ye scribe, after which Prof. H. C. Simmons[2] made an interesting talk. Dinner was announced, and of course all partook of the nice delicacies prepared for the occasion. The afternoon was spent pleasantly with the young people. Some took buggy rides, some seated themselves beneath the green willow trees beside the pond and, as the merry chirp of the little birds echoed among the gentle zephyrs of the trees, and as the beautiful streamlet rippled over the pebbles, seeming to say, "Welcome, friends, one and all," they told their sweet story of love, and ere the golden sun had bent low in the western skies, many a heart was made to rejoice and to exclaim that another pleasant day was numbered with the past.

Omitted from this lyrical account of young love in bloom, be it noted, was any reference to the presence of redbugs in the grass and ticks under those green willow trees.

The Christmas season was the time for parties, which were always held in the evening. The young people met by pre-

[1] This was Silas Horn, who two years later became the teacher of the community school at Shiloh Church.

[2] Professor Simmons was teacher of the school at Millerville, five miles away. He was at this time an elderly man with white whiskers and flashing eyes. He aspired to be a political leader in the county, but the majority of his fellow citizens distrusted him because of his radical opinions and unstable character.

arrangement in the parlor of a farmhouse and sat around a big log fire. At first the spirit of shyness hovered over the company, but soon the spell was broken. There were sallies of wit, or what passed for wit, and bursts of laughter. Shortly someone, bolder than the rest, suggested that they play "Animals," and the suggestion was unanimously adopted. Standing up, the self chosen leader then announced that his animal was the tabby cat, and he proceeded to assign an animal, preferably a malodorous one, to each of the others present. Then he said "I hug my tabby cat," and each of the others had to follow suit. Thus: "I hugged my billy goat," "I hugged my polecat," "I hugged my rhinoceros," and the like. It was simply too funny for anything; but hilarity reached the nth degree when the leader swapped slobber with his tabby cat.

Another game was called "Grunts." In this game the boys and girls, standing up, formed a ring around the room. Inside the ring stood a boy (we will say), blindfolded and holding a broom. Those forming the ring marched around in time to some sort of rhythmical chant. When the blindfolded boy reached out with the broom and touched a person in the ring, the marching stopped and the fun began. The person touched took the loose end of the broom and held it near his or her mouth and grunted, "Ugh." Blindfold, with the other end of the broom near his mouth, grunted in reply: Ugh, Ugh; Woof, Woof; Meow, Meow. There is a smothered giggle, followed by a general laugh. So it's a girl. Blindfold guesses it is Mary. Burst of laughter. He is mistaken; it was Sally. So the marching and the chanting are resumed, and the grunting is repeated, until blindfold guesses the right person. Whereupon the person thus identified exchanges places with blindfold, and the game goes on.

Still another game was called "Lovers." In this game boys and girls formed a ring around the room. Inside the ring stood a boy (we will say), with all his visual faculties unimpaired. Those forming the ring clapped their hands in rhythm and sang:

> Stand forth and face your lover
> Stand forth and face your lover
> Stand forth and face your lover
> The sweetest in the land

Whereupon the boy inside the ring stepped forward, faced the girl of his choice, and knelt before her as the others sang the next stanza:

> I kneel because I love you
> I kneel because I love you
> I kneel because I love you
> The sweetest in the land

Act one ends when the girl thus faced and knelt-to exchanges places with the boy inside the ring.

"Lovers" was an amusing game, full of banter and raillery; but it also had its romantic possibilities. I still remember how, at a Christmas party, an attractive little girl named Mary Prickett — God bless her memory — faced me in the ring and knelt because she loved me. Suddenly the room was filled with stardust, the melody of singing birds, and aroma from the spicy shores of Arabie the Blest.

> Of course 'twas puppy love, yet still
> To feel once more that fresh wild thrill

I'd give — But who can live youth over?[1]

A good game with which to end the party, around ten or eleven o'clock, was "Twistification," which bore some resemblance to dancing; but of course it could not be called dancing, because in our community the Terpsichorean art was severely frowned upon and denounced as a cardinal sin. All that "Twistification" amounted to was a spirited romp around the room, with boy swinging girl, and vice versa, first on one arm and then on the other.

A diversion was sometimes created at Christmas parties by the presence of Jasper Campbell with his fiddle. Jasper was a middle-aged farmer, shy and modest in his comportment, who accepted invitations to parties only under heavy pressure. His repertory was extensive, but "Arkansas Traveller" was his favorite piece. While playing this piece, he would stay his hand at intervals and, in a drawling voice, speak what purported to be the words of the song. Thus: "Old ummern (woman), look under the bed and get fully half that squirrel and cook it." Then he would resume his sawing as if he were playing the tune that fitted the words. How we laughed at that! Presently, to vary the entertainment, one of the boys, who was practiced in the art, would extract a heavy straw from the homemade broom in the corner and beat a rhythmical tattoo on the strings of the fiddle while Jasper continued to saw. We called that performance "beating straws." It was supposed to improve the quality of the music.

Weddings were family affairs, but the community was always agog with interest and curiosity when such an event

[1] With apologies to Edmund Clarence Stedman (1833-1908).

was in prospect. No formal announcements were ever sent out, but neighbors and friends who had observed the progress of the courtship could not easily be kept in the dark.

The wedding usually took place in the early evening at the home of the bride. Invited by word of mouth to be present were the relatives and intimate friends of the happy couple. At about six o'clock the preacher took his stance in the parlor with his back toward the fireplace; the guests crowded into the room; and slowly from the living room across the hallway came the loving pair, the lady clinging to her man's arm. They stopped a yard or so inside the parlor door, facing the preacher, who began the solemn and impressive words of the ceremony. After he had pronounced them man and wife, there was a moment of embarrassed silence, which was shortly broken by the cheerful voices of the young people, who crowded about the happy couple with congratulations and kisses. All the while the mother of the bride had been silently weeping — what for was anybody's guess.

There was never any joyful act of cutting the wedding cake or of tossing the bride's bouquet, but the lavish spread of victuals in the dining room after the ceremony made up for any deficiencies that an observer of the present day might call attention to.

By ten o'clock the married guests and their sleepy children were on their way home, but many of the gay young people were likely to linger a little longer to enjoy a bit of horseplay at the expense of the newlyweds. When the hour of bedtime arrived, for instance, the young ladies of the party, with giggles and laughter, might lay hands on the protesting bride, drag her into the parlor, and put her to bed. When the young ladies emerged from the room, the young men would drag the embarrassed bridegroom in and put him to bed beside his blushing bride. The parlor door would then be closed, and the frolicksome young people, with the sense of having done something naughty and clever, would go home also.

The next day the infare took place at the home of the groom's parents. All the wedding guests were expected to be there in time for the big feast at noon. Before sundown the entertainment was over and the guests had departed. The newlyweds usually made the home of the groom's parents their temporary abode until they could buy furniture and start housekeeping for themselves. They returned to the home of the bride's parents occasionally for short visits; they traveled about a good deal within a radius of ten or twelve miles, stopping as guests, sometimes as self-invited guests, at the homes of relatives and friends; but they never went away by themselves on a honeymoon, in the present day meaning of that term.

Spring was the season for log-rolling.

In the Hatchet Creek community when I was a boy, it was the general practice of enterprising farmers to expand their cultivable acreage during the winter months by encroaching a little further upon the primeval forest. Small trees and underbrush were cut down and piled up to be burned without the assistance of neighbors; but large trees were only girdled, or "deadened," by cutting through the sapwood around each tree, and allowed to stand. Trees thus girdled fell down in three or four years, when their trunks and heavy limbs had to be cut into pieces of convenient length, piled into heaps, and burned. The piling of these heavy logs into heaps was called log-rolling, though it might more accurately be called log-toting, and it required the help of neighbors.

The principal implement used at log-rollings was the hand-pole, or hand-stick, cut from a small sapling, usually a dogwood, and dressed to proper shape with a drawing knife. It was about six feet long and from three to four inches in diameter at the middle. It tapered gradually from the middle toward each end, and at the ends it measured about an inch in diameter.

The logs to be rolled were from ten to fifteen feet long, and many of them were from three to four feet in diameter. The hand-poles were thrust under the log and the men took positions on opposite sides of the log, a man to each end of every hand-pole; and they simply lifted the log by main strength and carried it to the log heap. Such lifting strained every muscle in the body. I have seen a dozen strong men straighten up with a log that was heavier than they could carry and for several seconds stand under the fearful strain, unable to take a single step, until other men with hand-poles could come to their assistance. Sometimes a man at one end of a hand-pole could not rise with his burden. Then there was a general guffaw from the crowd, and the reputation for physical prowess of his partner at the other end of the hand-pole soared. All men coveted the prestige that fell to the man who could "pull down" any man in the community in a log-tote.

While the men were thus engaged in the "new ground,"

their womenfolk were of course at the farmhouse helping the hostess prepare the enormous meal and also stitching for her the quilt which hung in its frame from the ceiling in the parlor. At noon the dinner horn was blown as the signal for the men to drop their hand-poles and come and get it.

After the heavy logs had been piled in the new ground, the neighbors went home feeling that they had spent a delightful day and at the same time rendered a valuable service to a good neighbor who would always stand ready and willing to serve them in return.

Roads in the Hatchet Creek community were narrow and winding and, in many places, choked with mud. With careful maneuvering, two cotton wagons could pass each other at most places; but after a year of wear and tear and heavy rains, these community thoroughfares were in sore need of repair.

For the repair of roads in the county, the voting precinct, called the "beat," was taken as a convenient area. Each year the Court of Commissioners sitting at the county seat under the chairmanship of the Probate Judge appointed a resident citizen of each beat as road overseer and made him responsible, without any monetary compensation, for the upkeep of the roads within his beat.

Hatchet Creek community lay within the boundaries of two beats — Coleta and Brownville. Each summer, after the crops were laid by, the overseer for each beat warned all able-bodied men within his jurisdiction, who were between the ages of eighteen and forty-five, to appear on a certain day at a designated place for the repair of the roads, and each man was warned to bring with him a shovel or a hoe or an ax or perhaps a plowing outfit. Failure to heed the warning of the overseer, without a good excuse, was a serious offense.

The road work in each beat was usually carried on at different places simultaneously by two or three groups of men organized as working units, the overseer passing from one group to another and giving directions. Plows were used to open the ditches on each side of the road, and crude, wooden drags, distant ancestors of the modern bulldozer, were used to pile the loose dirt into the middle of the road. The problem of drainage was a difficult one and was never satisfactorily solved, but shallow ditches across the road, sometimes spanned by small bridges, offered temporary solution. In the miry bottomlands pine poles were laid down in long panels of corduroy and then buried beneath a slushy covering of mud.

Working the road, without monetary compensation from the county or the state, was commonly regarded as a necessary but hateful task. The men engaged in it were never aflame with a desire to work hard and do a satisfactory job. On the contrary, many of them loafed shamelessly, leaning on the handles of their hoes and shovels, sitting in the shade of the trees, discussing politics or the condition of the crops, chewing tobacco and indulging in slimy talk, scuffling with one another and sometimes fighting. The overseer, who was usually a man of some experience and strength of character, often had to take the lead and do much of the work with his own hands, in order to set an example for the others to follow. Of course he was just one of the neighbors and as such he could not well afford to exert his legal authority. Moral suasion was the best weapon in his armory.

Ten days a year was all the law exacted of a man for the repair of the roads. If for any reason he did not desire to serve in person, he was permitted to send a substitute.

By reason of all these various activities, the inhabitants of the Hatchet Creek community came to know one another and to intermingle socially.

POLITICS

DURING THE YEARS when I was passing from childhood to adolescence, I heard much complaint about the sad plight of the farmer, who paid such high prices for the goods he needed and received such low prices for the cotton he sold. How could the farmer pay his debts to the merchant in the fall unless the price of cotton went up and the price of goods went down?

Pa frequently discussed in my hearing the political and economic condition of the country, and naturally I accepted his conclusions as authoritative and definitive. If I understood him aright, he was saying that what we needed to extricate ourselves from the oppression of the merchant in the South and the big moneyed man in the North was free coinage of silver at the ratio of sixteen to one. I did not comprehend the meaning of this magic formula, of course, but I had not the slightest doubt that in it lay the solution of all our problems.

When the Farmers' Alliance movement struck Clay County around 1888, Pa was inclined to give it his full approval. He attended a few meetings of the local unit at nearby Brownville and listened to the speeches, but he could not become a member of the Alliance because the religious denomination to which he belonged strictly forbade its members to join secret societies. Two or three years later, when the Alliance blossomed out as the People's Party and gave its support to the candidacy of Reuben F. Kolb for the Governorship, Pa backed away from the radical movement, as did Asa Blair, John Rozelle, and many another stanch Democrat in the community, and pronounced it anathema.

In 1892 the People's Party ran a ticket in Clay County and elected all its candidates: E. A. Phillips as Probate Judge, F. M. Monroe as Sheriff, J. A. Bell as Tax Collector, and others. But the gloom that settled down on stanch Democrats was shortly dispelled by the glad tidings that Grover Cleveland had been elected President of the United States and that Reuben F. Kolb had been defeated by Thomas G. Jones in the race for the Governorship of the state.

When the news of these Democratic victories in high places reached the Hatchet Creek community, the announcement went forth that there would be a torchlight procession along the Goodwater-Talladega road from Frank Rozelle's store to the schoolhouse at Shiloh Church, a distance of about two miles. On the night appointed for the demonstration, a score of marchers, mostly young men, armed with muzzle loading shotguns, cow bells, and other noise-making apparatus, gathered at the store. In the hip pockets of several marchers were also small flasks of "Oh-be-joyful." The chief item on the program was a rip-roaring serenade of Tull Goza, who was the outstanding leader of the People's Party in the community and whose wife kept the postoffice. The serenade took place as scheduled. Shotguns boomed and cow bells clanged to the accompaniment of Indian war whoops. But after the serenade was over there was an anti-climax. Before the procession reached the schoolhouse, it degenerated into a series of ugly brawls among the marchers, thanks to corn liquor and the exuberant spirit of youth, and disbanded without ceremony.

But after all our rejoicing Cleveland soon displayed the glistening back of a "gold bug," and we turned away from him in disgust.

By 1894 the country was in the throes of an industrial and agricultural depression. Thousands of unemployed workingmen, under the leadership of "General" Coxey, marched from the Middle West into Washington and were forbidden by the minions of the law to trample on the grass; strikes tied up railroads in and around Chicago, and Cleveland sent federal troops to the area to suppress the labor disturbances and keep the trains running; in the South cotton sold at five cents a pound.

During the summer of 1894 Alabama was the scene of a lively struggle between the Bourbon Democrats and the Populists, as members of the People's Party were called, for the control of the state. The Democratic candidate for Governor was William C. Oates; the Populist candidate, Reuben F. Kolb.

The spirit of the campaign permeated the homes, the schools, the churches, and every form of social organization . . . Kolb clubs and Oates clubs were organized, and people assembled in throngs to be regaled by campaign orators who declaimed with the fervor of camp-meeting evangelists. Every club was a center of propaganda, and its rendezvous was bedecked with appropriate emblems — corn cobs, displayed in manifold ways, informing even the casual observer that he was at a Kolb camp, and oats on similar exhibition announced to the onlooker that he was on Oates ground. At public gatherings Kolb supporters appeared with walking sticks and pipes made of corn cobs, and they bedecked their horses, wagons, and buggies with cobs. The Oates men, not to be outdone, wore hatbands and belts made of oats or fastened oats under their hatbands and in the lapels of their coats, and in other ways demonstrated their position in the campaign. At every form of public meeting could be heard the yells "Hurrah for Kolb" and "Hurrah for Oates." Schools were noisy with such shouts.[1]

Oates was declared elected, but the supporters of Kolb, with very good reason, cried fraud and refused to acquiesce. The inaugural ceremony took place on the steps of the state-house at Montgomery under the protection of a cordon of troops ordered out by the retiring Governor, Thomas G. Jones. Simultaneously the supporters of Kolb, at a convenient distance, went through the formality of inaugurating their candidate also — on a wagon in the street. All this excitement made good copy for the newswriters, but no blood was shed. In later days Democrats admitted that Kolb had received the majority of the votes cast in the election; but they claimed, with sly winks, that Kolb's votes were not of the right quality.

Under date of May 18, 1894, the *Clay County Advance* published the following:

---

[1] A. B. Moore, *History of Alabama* (1934), pp. 726-737.

Mr. M. B. Garrett was nominated by acclamation by a un-
animous vote, there being no other name before the convention. Mr. Garrett not being present, a committee composed
of Asa Blair, John Rozelle, and Dudley Glass was appointed to
notify Mr. Garrett of his nomination and insist upon his acceptance of the same.

The office for which Pa had been nominated was that of
county representative to the state legislature, and the nomi-
nating agency was the county Democratic convention sitting
at Ashland.

One day the notifying committee rode up to our front
gate on horseback and called Pa out for an interview. Several
other persons, including myself, gathered around to hear
what was said. Pa insisted that he did not have the proper
qualifications for such an important office, that he was only
a poor farmer and humble minister of the Gospel, that he was
not the man to sling mud in a hot political campaign; to which
the committee replied that the Democrats of the county, in
convention assembled, had unanimously tagged him for the
job and that he could not afford to let them down. The interview ended with Pa's acceptance of the nomination and his
agreement to make a vigorous canvass of the county for votes.
On June 1 the *Clay County Advance* came out with Pa's
name printed on the Democratic ticket, and the race was on.

Early in July, as luck would have it, my brother Warner
fell desperately ill and had to have his leg amputated. For
days he hovered between life and death. So Pa's presence
was sorely needed at home and his promise to canvass the
county for votes could not be kept.

Meanwhile, Pa's Populist opponent, Joe Manning, a young

man in his early twenties, with the physcial appearance of a school boy, was canvassing the county vigorously, denouncing Grover Cleveland and the Democratic Party, and slinging mud at poor Pa.

A few years earlier Pa had sold twenty-five bushels of corn at a dollar a bushel to a Negro, named Plez Adair, who lived on a little farm in The Glades, between Hatchet Creek and Millerville, and had taken a mortgage on Plez's corn crop to insure the payment of the debt. When the debt came due and no payment was forthcoming, Pa foreclosed the mortgage and took fifty bushels of poor Plez's nubbins, because in the meanwhile the price of corn had dropped to fifty cents a bushel.

The Populists got hold of this story, embellished it considerably, invented a few others to match it, and came out with loud denunciations of "Brother Garrett" as an extortioner, as an oppressor of the poor, a robber of widows and orphans, a wolf in sheep's clothing.

One day the *People's Party Advocate*, published at Ashland, came out with two crude pictures labeled "Bro. Garrett." One represented Pa creeping up on a young buzzard crouched on a low stump; the other showed the Devil riding "Bro. Garrett" all over Hell. There seemed to be no point to the scurvy jest except to make Pa appear ridiculous.

When the votes were counted at the end of the election, it was discovered that Manning had a majority of forty-seven. Pa brushed the mud from his political garments as best he could and declared that never again could he be dragged into another mess like that.

During the season of hot politics in 1894, someone distributed in the Hatchet Creek community free copies of a cheap, paper-covered book entitled *Coin's Financial School*, which advocated the free coinage of silver at the ratio of sixteen to one. Nearly everybody thumbed through the book, even the children. I could not follow the argument; I bogged down in the statistics; but I could understand the pictures. Here was the picture of an immense cow superimposed upon the map of the United States. Her head was in Kansas and her hindparts in New England. Energetic Western farmers were feeding the cow great quantities of hay and grain, while a disconsolate Southern farmer sat nearby on a bale of cotton labeled "7 cents." At the other end of the cow pig-faced gentlemen in top hats and long coats milked the cow and carried away the milk in huge pails labeled with dollar marks. On another page of the book was the picture of a huge octopus-like creature, labeled Rothschilds, with tentacles wrapped around all the countries of the globe. Now here was something concrete and comprehensible: the farmer and the industrial laborer did all the work, but those pig-faced gentlemen up North got all the gravy.

In the midst of our despair over the sad political and economic condition of the country, a silvery voice came to us from out of the West, saying: "Thou shalt not press down upon the brow of labor a crown of thorns; thou shalt not crucify mankind on a cross of gold."

The Presidential campaign of 1896 had in it all the elements of a religious crusade. When the sad news arrived that William Jennings Bryan, "the boy orator of the Platte," had gone down in defeat, that good Christian had succumbed to the darts of Apollyon, one fifteen year old boy, recently of the Hatchet Creek community, was thoroughly convinced that our beloved country, sweet land of liberty, was Hell bent, and fast.

AND NOW GOODBYE

ON OUR FARM in the Hatchet Creek community there were out-croppings of pyrites. In the summer of 1895 Pa sold the farm to a mining company for the fancy price of $3,000 and bought another farm near Lineville, twenty miles away.

During the fall and winter of 1895 we were occupied at convenient intervals with the transportation of our food products and farm equipment to the new home. My brother Warner and I were entrusted with the responsibility of the first load — two heavy barrels of sorghum molasses on a wagon drawn by two mules. Before we reached Millerville, six miles away, the jolting of the wagon had loosened the hoops on one of the barrels; molasses soon covered the floor of the wagon bed and, trickling through the cracks, left a sticky trail along the road. We did our level best to drive the hoops back into place with blows from sharp-edged rocks, but to no avail. At Monroe's mill we stopped and told our tale of woe to a kind-hearted blacksmith, who, within an hour, fashioned heavy hoops from discarded wagon tires and drove them into place on the barrel while the iron was still hot. In measure as the new hoops cooled off they contracted and closed the crevices in the barrel. We asked the blacksmith what he charged for his services. He replied, "Nothing at all." He was happy, he said, to do a small favor for the sons of "Brother Garrett."

When the time finally arrived to break camp and move our household goods, Cousin John Carpenter and Mr. John Moon, who were to be our next door neighbors in our new home, came with their wagons to give us a lift and thereby show their neighborly spirit. They spent the night with us. Early the next morning Garrett Carpenter, Cousin John's son, and I started out on foot driving our two milk cows along the road. The idea was that shortly the wagons would catch up with us and take us aboard, and someone else would be designated to drive the cows for a while.

All went well with Garrett and me for nearly a mile. The cows ambled along docilely as good cows are supposed to do, but on reaching the outer limits of the free range where they were accustomed to wander in quest of pasture, they became restless and eventually raised their tails and galloped off into the open forest of tall pines. For several minutes Garrett and I bestirred ourselves in an effort to head them off and turn them back into the road; but a footrace between a cow and a boy is a rather lopsided affair. Garrett soon threw up the sponge and strongly advised that we cease our exertions; but I knew that those cows had to be turned back into the road. So with aching lungs and exhausted legs I continued the race and, by dint of throwing rocks at the animals and yelling bloody murder, I succeeded at long last in my efforts. When the wagons came up with us, the cows were again ambling along the road. As I look back over the years to that incident, I think there is a moral lesson to be drawn from my conduct on that occasion, but I am far too modest to explain what it is.

And now goodbye to the horse and buggy days on Hatchet Creek.

The lapse of years finds me and my wife ensconced in an old, renovated farmhouse in upstate New York, just twenty miles from the St. Lawrence river. From our front porch in the summertime I can look out over rolling meadows and pasturelands all carpeted with green. In the meadows dairy farmers are cutting and baling hay and harvesting grain with machinery. Not a horse in sight. In the pasturelands herds of pure-bred cattle are grazing — Holsteins, Jerseys, Guernseys, or Ayrshires. Huge trucks, as big as railway box cars roll along the paved highways, bringing food products from far away places — from Florida, from California, from the four corners of the earth. In the grocery stores of the nearby villages of Canton and Potsdam, my wife can buy tropical fruits and spring vegetables at any time of the year. When our daughter wants to come home for a week end, she phones from Rochester, two hundred miles away, and we meet her at the train or the bus station in our Plymouth. After the evening meal, which we still call supper, we sit by the radio and listen to the news broadcasts, laugh at the comedies of Jack Benny and Amos 'n' Andy, or enjoy various sorts of music. Some of our neighbors have television sets, though the reception is not good in this area. One evening not long ago two neighbors of ours, man and wife, who live on a dairy farm hardly a mile away, dropped in to tell us of their wonderful trip around the world. They flew from San Francisco to

Sydney, Australia, and returned by boat to England and thence to New York City.

All our neighbors are interesting and some are well-informed. When they call on us or we call on them, there is much talk of the existing international tension, of the possibilities inherent in nuclear energy, of the prospect of a third World War, of the danger of creeping inflation, of the plight of the poor dairy farmer who has to pay such high prices for the commodities he needs and who receives such low prices for the milk he sells; of the shortcomings of the rising generation, boys and girls who flee the farm as soon as they are grown and betake themselves to the city in quest of easier work and shorter hours; of the corruption in politics and the wickedness of people in general; of the unwisdom of public assistance to paupers, the majority of whom could earn a living for themselves if only they were compelled to do so. In short, I get the impression from talking with my neighbors that the conditions of life now-a-days are much worse than they used to be.

As I listen to such talk, I recall having read somewhere about a cuneiform tablet dug up by a group of archeologists in the ruins of an ancient city in the Near East, a city which had ceased to exist two thousand years before the birth of Christ. When the inscription on the tablet was deciphered it was found to read as follows: "Children no longer obey their parents; the world is coming to an end; everybody is trying to write a book."

And so it must have ever been.

My granddad, viewing earth's worn cogs,

Said things were going to the dogs;
His granddad in his house of logs,
Said things were going to the dogs;
His granddad in the Flemish bogs,
Said things were going to the dogs;
His granddad in his old skin togs,
Said things were going to the dogs;
There's one thing that I have to state:
The dogs have had a good long wait.

ANONYMOUS[1]

---

[1] Lifted from *Good Housekeeping* (January, 1954), p. 4.